GL

Ira Trivedi is the bestselling author of four books, most recently of *India in Love*, a seminal work of non-fiction on India's social revolution and sexual violence. Her first novel, *What Would You Do to Save the World* was published when she was eighteen to critical and commercial success. Ira is a contributor to Foreign Affairs, Foreign Policy and several others where her work on gender and culture has won several awards. She has been called one of India's most important youth voices and she speaks regularly to media and forums in India and internationally. She recently won the UK media award for her story on bride trafficking and was honoured at the House of Lords in England.

When Ira is not writing she is teaching yoga. She is the founder of the NGO Namami Yoga and most recently she led the first international yoga day celebrations at Rajpath, New Delhi where 36,000 people including the prime minister of India did yoga creating a world record.

GUMRAH

11 Short Teen Crime Stories

Based on tele-series *Gumrah* by Star India Pvt. Ltd

Ira Trivedi

Foreword by
Chetan Bhagat

RUPA

Published by
Rupa Publications India Pvt. Ltd 2016
7/16, Ansari Road, Daryaganj
New Delhi 110002

Sales centres:
Allahabad Bengaluru Chennai
Hyderabad Jaipur Kathmandu
Kolkata Mumbai

ISBN: 978-81-291-3955-9

Third impression 2016

10 9 8 7 6 5 4 3

The moral right of the author has been asserted.

Printed at HT Media Ltd, Noida

To the Indian youth.
You are the future of this country,
the beacon of our hope.

Contents

᠀

Foreword

Human beings are social animals. To interact with other people is almost our basic need. We need to engage with other humans in order to live our lives. This necessitates the need for us to trust others, and let them in our lives. However, we humans also have another need. We need to feel safe. Which means we cannot trust just about anyone and everyone. For if we are not careful about whom we trust, we could be used or even harmed.

It is the above two contradicting needs that drive much of our social lives. To have lots of people in our lives, but to also remain safe. These two conflicting needs also makes it important for all of us to have a good sense of judgment about people. Does the other person deserve my trust? It is not an easy question to answer. Sometimes, it takes decades to be able to gain the wisdom of choosing people wisely. Sometimes, even decades are not enough. Some of us are more trusting by nature and so we fall into the same traps and heartbreaks again and again.

The situation becomes even more pronounced at a young age, when you are in your teens and twenties. You have just come out of the protection of childhood and the responsibility of choosing people is thrust upon you. Your hormones rage, your desire to be popular peaks, and your judgment is not yet formed. In such a scenario, it is easy to get swayed by what seems tempting and risk-free, while in reality it is not.

The problem is that there is no one set of rules that one can follow to remain safe, and yet enjoy a good social life. Each case is different, and requires a keen sense of judgment. Hence, one can learn more from actual stories and cases, than from a list of preachy do's and don'ts.

This is where this book comes in. *Gumrah*, consisting of stories based on an already popular TV series, are all stories of when someone took advantage of someone's trust or poor judgment, in real life. Sometimes the consequences were a nasty lesson for the victim, and sometimes far more disastrous.

The purpose of this book (or the TV series) is not to scare you, far from it. It is merely to tell you of the dangers out there, if you don't keep your wits around you. In most stories, you will see the early signs of upcoming trouble were there, but because the victim was so lost in the moment, he or she couldn't keep an eye out for them.

In your life too, most times, things will be safe and there would be no reason to worry. However, there may be a rare time when something will alert you. The situation may be different from what is mentioned in these stories, but certain aspects—early warning signs, unanswered questions and chance of potential trouble will be there. If that happens, seek help, tell others and protect yourself well before it is too late.

I congratulate Channel V for their successful show, which is not only entertaining to watch, but also serves a purpose in today's society. I also congratulate Ira Trivedi, for translating the episodes of the show into easy-to-read stories, that people can now carry with them and read them over time.

I wish you all the best.

Stay social. Stay safe.

Chetan Bhagat

Soulmate

I.

1 May 2012, Asha Mental Institute, Nagpur

While growing up, Pankhuri and I were best friends. As close as close can be—like peas in a pod, Mama used to joke. Pankhuri was not only my younger sister; she was also my best friend, my soulmate, my constant companion. It's still difficult for me to understand how such a deep, soul-binding relationship could have self-detonated, ruining forever not only our lives, but also the lives of all those around us.

Sad to say, the insecurity was triggered off by the way we looked, or rather, the way that *I* looked. But I suspect, and Dr Patel tells me so, that there must have been something larger at play, something which had built up over the years, which led me to act in that crazed, horrendous way which I eventually did. Even though I think hard about what could have possibly gone wrong between us, I still cannot figure out how the beautiful bond that I had enjoyed with my little sister since the day she was born, could have gone sour over the course of just one year. Dr Patel tells me that things must have happened in our childhood, things that had sowed the seeds of hate which created that all-consuming demon.

Sometimes, when I think back, plumbing deep into the recesses of my memory, I can remember things or at least I can imagine them. I remember Pankhuri as being fairer, cuter, more lovable. Being pampered by my parents while I sat on the floor watching them pamper her and show her off to relatives and visitors. I remember her being fed by my mother while I whined, hungry for her breast. But, she was younger than me, and always got more attention than I had ever had.

As we grew older, I recall more vividly than anything else my father favouring her—the lively, endearing child—while my heart ached silently with longing for his love, and the wish to be adored the way Pankhuri was. But Papa did not care for the qualities I possessed; he didn't care that I stood first in class, or that I won the English essay competition, or that my teachers told me that I had the potential of becoming a star debater. To him, those things didn't matter; to him it was important that we should be fair-skinned, slim-hipped, eligible daughters who could be married off to rich husbands who would care for them for the rest of their lives.

The bad times started when Papa took a new job

in Indore. In Meerut, at the small all-girls' school that we attended, Pankhuri and I shared everything—snacks, friends, uniforms. But when we moved, Papa's new job allowed us to go to a big, prestigious co-ed school. To Pankhuri, the thought was exciting. Boys! How marvellous it would be! Even before we started school, she had stars in her eyes as she dreamt up all sorts of Bollywood-style love stories with her playing the lead role. I felt differently; the thought of boys scared me so much that it literally gave me goosebumps. I had no brothers, had never grown up with male cousins, and the only male characters in my life were Papa and Dadaji. And those two...I doubted very much that the boys in our school would be like them. Pankhuri could sense my apprehensions, even though I never really spoke to her about them.

'Di, boys are just like girls. Except cuter,' she would say with a giggle. 'Don't worry, school will be a lot more fun with them; you just wait and watch.'

But her words didn't do a thing for me. I still worried and, in my fear and anxiety, I did what I always did when I got stressed out. I started eating more and sticking my head into my books, preparing myself for the 11th standard. I knew that my new school would be a lot more competitive than my school in Meerut; and I was determined to stand first in my class, as I had been my entire life.

It was during that summer that Pankhuri and I slowly started growing apart. She devoted all her time to readying herself for a co-ed world. She dieted, trimmed her skirts to show off her long legs; and she was constantly doing something or the other to her hair. She watched American television sitcoms in which high-school girls led glamorous lives and indulged in sizzling romances. I, on the other hand, read novels, ate junk food, gained weight and studied.

Things became worse after we started school. Pankhuri quickly fit in: she made friends, joined the basketball team and, for a change, even did well in her studies. Everyone seemed to take to her spontaneously; she was easy-going, pretty, funny. What was there not to like her? It wasn't so simple for me. I found it difficult to make friends. I was awkward around boys, tongue-tied whenever someone tried to talk to me, and I was no good in sports. Even my marks plummeted. In Meerut I had *always* been number one; but here, I had to struggle to keep afloat.

For the first time, Pankhuri and I disagreed over something: she loved Indore Public School (IPS), I hated it. Pankhuri thrived here; she had a whole new group of friends, she had boys running after her. The basketball coach said she showed great possibilities which, maybe, she had had all along. Although my marks were picking up, I was spending most of my time studying. I grew more and more depressed, and I isolated myself even more from my beloved sister and any friends I could have made.

At IPS, I became conscious of the way I looked. Maybe that is what boys do to you. They make you conscious of every little part of your body. Never before had the hair on my legs, or my eyebrows bothered me. In fact, I had never even noticed that I had hair above my lip. Suddenly, at IPS, everything about the way I looked began to bother me. I also started to notice how beautiful Pankhuri was. She had perfect hair, thick and silky, with the bounce of a rubber ball. She didn't have hair between her eyebrows or above her lip; she was fair and had a beautiful complexion, which became a peony pink after basketball practice. As for her figure, the more I noticed how shapeless my body was, the more I realized how perfect hers was—lithe and thin, curved in the right places. She had the body of a girl with the grace of a woman. As for me, potato was the first word that came to mind. When I looked at Pankhuri, radiant and happy, I wondered how two people who looked *so* different could be sisters.

Even now, I look into the mirror at my dull, dark-skinned face and I often think to myself: if I had been beautiful, slim and fair like Pankhuri, maybe, I would not have turned into the monster that I became. Maybe, I would not have clobbered my sister to death.

2.

3 May, 12 p.m.

Dr Patel has explained to me that it is important to analyse every detail, every event, every spoken word, every single feeling that I had which might be connected to the incidents of that day. He has told me to picture everything; to create a scenario in my mind of all the happenings and the people that led to that day.

It began with Sujith. By the 12th standard, I had settled

into my own darkness. In a strange way, I had accepted it, and I even had a faint sense of what it might be like to be happy. I did what I could to keep myself from going over the edge, though I realize only now, how close to it I really was. I studied hard, and kept at it, slowly making my way to the top of the class. I had hardly any friends, nor was I was part of any extra-curricular activity that would have helped me make friends. Pankhuri and I kept drifting further and further apart. Unlike me, everything she touched turned to gold, and she became everyone's favourite—from my parents to the headmistress—while I was relegated to the shadows.

It was at this time that Sujith came into my life. He charged into that dull classroom like a tidal wave, and I drowned in his glory. I had never before felt like that about a boy, and I wondered how it was even *possible* to feel that way. Nervous and happy, anxious and excited, scared and hopeful—all at the same time. I had had crushes on boys over the past year; crushes that I had soon squashed, or that had died a quick and natural death. But this—this was something totally different. It was as if Sujith had permeated every cell of my body. No matter what I did, I just couldn't stop thinking about him. He was always there, somewhere at the back of my mind. And I had never spoken to him. I doubt that he had even seen me, though he sat only four seats away. Why would he? After all, why would this tall, handsome, dignified, intelligent person *ever* notice a potato like me?

One day, all that changed. Mr John, our physics teacher,

asked me to coach Sujith. I was his best student, and Sujith had joined school half-way through the school year on account of his father's transfer. Mr John considered Sujith a bright student; but he had missed out on many fundamentals, which he wanted me to teach him. He asked me whether I could spare some time to bring Sujith up to scratch. I almost fainted. All I could do was look at him in dumbfounded silence with my mouth hanging open way down to my knees. I finally mustered a tiny nod, and so Sujith became my student. I teaching *Sujith*, and him learning from *me*. It was totally unexpected; a dream come true, almost too good to believe.

It was strange in the beginning to say the least. I grew warm and flushed whenever he was close to me. Since I was incapable of coherent communication, in the first few lessons, I would write in a notebook while he watched me. But of course, things could not progress this way; and I didn't want Sujith thinking I was a total moron, so I quickly got my act together and prepared an excellent study-plan, which undoubtedly impressed him. And while we were studying quantum physics, the most unbelievable, unimaginable thing happened: for the first time, I became *friendly* with a *boy*. Sujith made me realize that what Pankhuri had once told me was correct—boys weren't all that bad. They were not at all like girls (in that, Pankhuri was wrong); but they were interesting in their own way, sometimes I felt, a lot more than even girls.

Gradually, what had started out as awkward tutorials ended up as friendship. I do not claim to having become best friends with him—or anything like that—but I did feel that I meant something to Sujith. In a strange way, his presence improved my relationship with my family. They respected me for taking on the responsibility of tutoring someone; somehow, that made them look at me a little differently. My relationship with Pankhuri too improved and she began to treat me as she used to in Meerut—an older sister to whom she looked up and whom she admired.

3.

I'm not sure when it started, and I blame myself for not noticing it earlier; but before I knew it, Pankhuri had joined us to make it a threesome. She would drop in at the end of the tuition, and the three of us would walk over to a tea-stall or to an ice cream stand. She had a way with people, and she always made us laugh. I could tell that Sujith liked her, but I thought it was only because she was my little sister. I did not realize that what I mistook for innocent fun was in fact two people falling in love. While I thought I was the connecting link between them, in reality, I was just getting in their way. I was, without knowing it, a bona fide *kabab mein haddi.*

I cannot recollect exactly when or how it dawned on me. Dr Patel keeps pressing me to remember because he says it is a critical point. What made me catch on to the fact that Sujith was in love with Pankhuri? Was it the way he looked at her? The way his eyes followed her wherever she went? The way he became soft and diffident around her; so different from the attentive, inquisitive, almost aggressive boy he was during our tuition? I am at a loss as to *what* it was that struck me, but when it did strike, I was stunned. I didn't know how to react. At this point, I didn't blame Pankhuri; after all she was not aware of how I felt about Sujith, nor of how much he liked her. I continued to think that she would hang out with us to re-bond with me, and make things the way they had been before IPS.

I had a burning desire for Sujith. I thought that maybe, just maybe if I told him how I felt, he would prevent himself from falling in love with her, and fall in love with me instead. That was what I was foolish enough to hope for.

So one evening, in the middle of solving a theorem, I kissed him. I don't know what came over me. He was sitting so close that I could smell the detergent in which his shirt had been washed. He was bent over, trying to solve a proof, and he turned to ask me a question; and there they were, right in front of me, his lips. I moved forward and I kissed him. His reaction remains a bit of a blur. I remember a look of shock, disbelief and then discomfort. He didn't leave or push me away; he just went back to solving the problem. When Pankhuri came to get us, he behaved as he always did around her: what I have now identified as textbook puppy love behaviour.

But the next day, he didn't come for tuition and he ignored me in class. He didn't come the next day either, or the day after that. I was broken; I didn't know what to do. I felt that I had made a terrible mistake. I blamed myself for being ugly, for being fat, for being stupid, for lacking self-control. I had probably lost him forever. Those three days, those seventy-two hours, when he ignored me were devastating. I didn't know it was possible for a heart to ache literally; but mine did, and it was painful in the strangest way. Just when I thought that things would never get better, Sujith showed up at my house asking to see me and it was as if a huge weight had been lifted from my heart.

Out of all my memories—many of which have been burnt away by anger, pain and grief—the memory of the walk that Sujith and I took remains crystal clear. It was a perfect winter afternoon; we had both taken off our blue school sweaters and tied them around the waist. It struck me that this was the first time I had spent time with him alone, outside of our tuition class, and the first time that we had spoken about something which didn't concern physics.

He walked faster than usual, and I had to struggle on my stubby legs to keep up with him. He talked seriously, with a harshness that I had never before heard from him; not once looking at me, but at the ground in front of him. I remember his words. They are engraved in my mind.

'Look, Pooja,' he said with a cold directness. 'I really appreciate all that you've down for me. I would never have even passed without your help. But I'm in a good place now. In the latest UT, I got only five marks less than you.'

I didn't know how to feel about this. Proud? Cheated? Jealous? Five marks behind me; that placed him among the top five students in the class.

'I won't be needing any more tuitions,' he said with a

finality. Then, after a pause, knowing that he had possibly hurt my feelings, he said, 'We will always be friends... good friends.' And then with some hesitation, 'You need to know that this has nothing to do with what happened the other day.'

I almost choked as I replayed that scene for the 1000th time in my head.

'That...that was a mistake, Pooja,' he continued a little more gently. 'I don't feel that way about you; and...and I don't think you do about me, either. I guess these things happen between friends,' he said.

I understood then just how hollow our relationship had been, and how deluded I had been about it. All those walks after our tuition, it had always been only him and Pankhuri. I had been the third person, just walking along with them. They were kind to me, as one is to a beggar, but beyond that I had meant nothing to Sujith.

He walked even faster now and I almost had to run to keep up with him. I didn't know what to say to him. Should I admit that I liked him? Or would that be a horrible mistake? Finally, I didn't have to say anything at all. Instead of walking me back home, as he always did when Pankhuri was with us, he told me he had to go back and we split ways. I didn't have a chance to say anything, but that was probably for the best.

4.

The next few weeks were some of the most unendurable

ones in my life, or at least that is how I felt at that time. I was lost without Sujith. Pankhuri and I grew distant as I withdrew into my old shell. My sweet sister did try her best to help me, but nothing could help me. Her untiring optimism wore me down and her brightness seemed to make my darkness even darker. I tried once again to get back on my feet, but it was more difficult than when I had first come to this school because I had tasted sweetness and happiness, and the taste of that elixir lingered on my tongue. Sujith's presence made it worse. Although I tried hard not to, I couldn't resist stealing glances at him in class, and I was astonished to see how happy and joyful he was. Sujith, like Pankhuri, had quickly assimilated into the school, and now that he was doing well on the academic front, he seemed to be more confident and self-assured than ever before. Like Pankhuri, he was always kind to me. He would smile at me and acknowledge me, and that was more than anyone else in class did for me. Just when things seemed to be at their worst, Raaghav arrived, as suddenly as Sujith disappeared.

5.

Dr Patel wants me to concentrate more on Raaghav. He tells me that Raaghav, despite being my partner in crime, was a positive influence in my life. That Raaghav, unlike most other people in my life, had made me feel good (or at least better) about myself. I keep telling Dr Patel that I don't want to think about Raaghav; that I want to forget him, that already some part of my mind has expunged his memory, that I can't quite remember him. Strange, because I had truly loved Raaghav, although in a different way than I had loved Sujith. It was less intense, but it was also more calming, more soothing, more peaceful. Raaghav had made me feel loved and appreciated and, for the first time in my life, I had been made to feel beautiful and that meant more than the world to me.

Raaghav and I had many things in common. Maybe the most important was that, like me, Raaghav was fat, shy and introverted. He had joined IPS at the same time as I, in the same standard, though in different sections. We met for the first time in the Chemistry Lab, an appropriate place for two geeks like us. Both of us had stayed back to finish our practical work, and as we struggled to make aspirin, we got talking. After Sujith, I had become a little more comfortable with boys, and I could at least carry on a half-way normal conversation. However, with Sujith I felt I was constantly under a magnifying glass, while with Raaghav I felt strangely at ease. I could be myself, and I didn't have to care about how I looked.

In the beginning, Raaghav and I would just work and study together, but over time we became good friends. I realized that he was as lonely as I was; that, like me, he didn't have many (or any) friends and he was desperate for companionship. Soon our friendship grew into something more and one day, as I was explaining a complex quadratic equation to him, he told me that he loved me. I told him that I too loved him. I assured him that I wasn't merely reciprocating his feelings, it was the honest truth. I *did* think I loved this shy, quiet boy who made me feel really special. But strange are the ways of the heart. I loved Raaghav and I felt happy with him, yet my heart would jump into my mouth every time I saw Sujith. I tried to avoid him as much as possible, but it was inevitable that I should see a lot of him considering he was in the same class as I and was dating my younger sister.

6.

I think back now to Pankhuri's birthday party, where matters came to a head. It was a small affair, nothing fancy; after all we weren't a fancy sort of a family, but we did the best that we could do. Mama baked a lovely cake, I made pizzas and French fries. We had music and games. Papa had bought both Pankhuri and me new outfits. Pankhuri looked ravishing in the lavender top and white capris that she had chosen, while I had opted for something more conservative. A long, loose black top, which covered my stomach, hips and thighs—my three problem areas. Pankhuri had lent me some earrings, gold danglers, on which everyone complimented me. Raaghav whispered in my ear that I looked like a princess, and I almost believed him until Sujith looked through me as if I were made of glass. He didn't even bother to say hello to me, although I was the one who had introduced him into our home. All through the evening, I was simmering inside but I maintained a calm facade. However, after two hours of holding in my anger, I could bear it no more. Only a few guests—Pankhuri's closest friends—stayed back, and so I went up to Sujith and tapped him on the shoulder.

'Remember me?' I said without a smile on my face.

'Hey! How are you? Uh...long time!' he said with a false grin plastered on his face.

'Not really. You've been here for two hours.'

'Uh yeah...just been busy with friends, I guess,' he said sheepishly.

'Didn't have the courtesy to come say hello?' I said, raising my voice a little to match my mood.

'No, no, nothing like that, yaar. Sorry, yaar. Was just busy you know. Too many people, you know. I just didn't see you,' Sujith replied.

'Didn't see me? Is that your excuse? How could you miss someone as FAT as me, huh?' I said, a little more aggressively than I had perhaps intended to.

'Didi?' said Pankhuri with concern. She had heard my raised voice and had come to see what was going on.

'Don't Didi me! Your boyfriend is a prick of the first order!'

'Sujith, is everything okay?' she asked, sounding concerned.

'God knows, yaar Panks. She's angry because I didn't come say hi to her. I was just busy with all of you yaar,' he complained, looking desperately at Pankhuri.

'Are you serious, Didi? Is that why you're angry?' Pankhuri asked, looking surprised.

'It's not that, it's just that I'm the one who brought this

guy into the house, and he doesn't even have the decency or politeness to say hello. He just looks through me as if I were made of glass. I know I'm not as hot as you, but still, this is my house too.'

'Di, have you gone crazy? It's my birthday party! Can't you control your insecurities for just ONE day?' she fumed, suddenly pulling him away with her as he looked embarrassed.

As I stood there, in semi-shock, Raaghav came to my side.

'What happened?' he asked with concern.

While I was narrating the incident to him, I felt that I had perhaps been over-sensitive. Instead of telling him the story as it had happened, I exaggerated a bit. I told him that Sujith was essentially an asshole who did not behave well with Pankhuri or me. Even today on her birthday he had been rude; that he had not even come to say hello to me though it was I who had first invited him into our home. I told him that I really did not like Sujith, and for my sister's sake, I wished that he would leave all of us alone.

Raaghav was touched by my concern for Pankhuri, but also taken aback by how much the incident seemed to have affected me. He took my hands and placed them on his chest.

'I promise that I shall put this guy right. You just watch and see.'

7.

Raaghav was chubby and geeky, but he was also strong and, as I discovered, a bit of a bully. I didn't take seriously what he had said about Sujith, because after all, what could Raaghav really do? It turned out that he could do quite a lot, especially when it came to boys like Sujith. I didn't believe him when he gleefully told me that he had beaten Sujith up and that the coward would never bother my sister or me again. Apparently, he had cornered Sujith after school, while he was on his way home. Raaghav had two iron rods and two of his friends with him. They beat up Sujith, not injuring him, but bruising him pretty badly. They threatened to use the iron rods if he came anywhere near the two of us in the future.

Then, a tearful Pankhuri told me that Sujith had stopped talking to her for no particular reason. No matter how much she reached out to him, he would not respond to her and he ignored her completely in school. She admitted that I had been right all along and that Sujith was a total asshole.

'It's just as you told him at the party,' she said glumly. 'He looks through me as if he's looking through a glass pane.'

'Never mind,' I told her, giving her a hug. 'He's an asshole. It's just as well you found that out sooner rather than later.'

'I'm really sorry, Di,' said Pankhuri as she burst into tears in my arms.

I did not feel an iota of guilt. In my mind, Sujith had

been mine first, and Pankhuri had stolen him away from me. It was my turn to take revenge, and now that I had, we were even, and we could go back to being normal. Dr Patel thinks that I was wrong in thinking this way, he thinks that I had been immature, that the way I had handled the situation with Raaghav and Sujith was childish. The truth is that I don't regret what Raaghav did, and I was happy that he had beaten up Sujith and driven him out of Pankhuri's life.

8.

Twelve hours that I have spent, twelve months, trying to erase from my memory, but each second, minute, hour of that day comes back to plague and haunt me just when I think that I'm getting better.

Pankhuri was in a dreadful, depressed mood and I was beginning to feel just a twinge of guilt. Thinking it would be good for her, I suggested that maybe Raaghav, she and I could spend a Sunday together, so she could get to know him better. She agreed immediately and seemed genuinely excited about visiting his farmhouse, an hour away from the city.

It was a lovely afternoon, perfect for spending a day outdoors. Pankhuri and I were both excited and spent a few hours getting ready for the trip, deciding what to wear, what to take with us, and packing a picnic basket with our favourite food.

I was a little anxious about what Pankhuri would

think of Raaghav. It was only natural that Pankhuri should compare the chubby, gauche Raaghav with the svelte and charming Sujith; but during the drive we chatted in an easy and friendly manner and I was glad to see that they were getting along well.

The last pleasant memory I have of that day is getting out of the car, stepping out onto a dirt road, and admiring the small cottage (not really a farmhouse) in the verdant surroundings, and the marvellous view. From that moment on, everything is a blur.

Dr Patel tells me that I must reconstruct those lost hours. It is crucial for me to understand what happened; but as much as I try, there are only a few things that come to mind.

I think that we ate, chatted, watched a movie (I even try to remember which one of the possible movies). Maybe, we even went for a walk before we decided to go for a swim in the small pool. As the hours passed, Raaghav and Pankhuri became friendlier, and the closer they got, the smaller I felt. Then there was the pool, and I vaguely remember Pankhuri taking off her jeans and top, and I remember the pink bikini that she wore underneath. I didn't know that she owned a bikini, leave alone that she had worn it to the farm. We had got ready together and she had said nothing about it. The one thing that I do remember distinctly despite the fog in my mind, is the look of affection and admiration on Raaghav's face when he saw her in that swimsuit. I am sure I will never forget that look.

By the time we were ready to drive back, Pankhuri and Raaghav were a little tipsy; they had both consumed the bottles of beer that Raaghav had brought. While we were packing the car, Pankhuri made a cute, funny comment and she and Raaghav laughed uncontrollably. She then went over and hugged Raaghav. I stared in silence and all I could think about at that moment was Sujith. Would Pankhuri steal Raaghav away from me as she had stolen Sujith? I don't know what came over me, but it was as if there was an uncontrollable demon of rage inside me, and before I even knew it, I had taken the iron rod which lay in the trunk of Raaghav's car—the same iron rod that he had used to threaten Sujith—and I was beating Pankhuri with it. She was screaming and Raaghav was trying to stop me, but I couldn't get myself to stop. I yelled mean harsh words at her that came from deep inside me; words that I couldn't have imagined that I would ever say to the sister I loved so much. I kept on beating her with all my strength till Raaghav managed to stop me, but by then, it was too late.

And then I collapsed on the ground next to my sister's body and cried.

I was told what happened after that. I don't remember though I had been a party to it. Raaghav and I realized that Pankhuri was dead. The iron rod had hit her head, cracked her skull and she had died on the spot. We pushed her body over the cliff, cleaned up the blood stains and drove home, promising each other that we would never talk about what had happened.

They tell me that I confessed everything almost immediately to the police: spending the day at the farmhouse, killing Pankhuri with the iron rod, and pushing her body over the cliff. I told them about my love for Sujith and how Raaghav had beaten him up. I feel that it is ironic that it was I, the perpetrator, who confessed, who gave us all away, not Raaghav, the abettor, nor Sujith.

I still don't understand why Raaghav helped to cover up my crime. I know he must have done it to keep me out of trouble, though there was very little that he could really do. I had killed my best friend, my sister, my soulmate, and I deserved to pay for my sin. But what makes life truly unbearable is the heavy burden of having involved Raaghav, of having ruined his life along with mine, when his only crime had been to love.

∽

I'll Burn Your Sister

The thick smoke from Kalpana's funeral pyre stung my eyes, finally bringing on a flood of tears; tears which, till now, had not come. It's not that I wasn't sad, I was devastated by the death of my younger, beloved sister—the person I loved most in the world. It's just that I was in a state of shock, and a numbness and sense of disbelief had taken over my entire being. Kalpu, dead? Kalpana, my beautiful sister with that magical smile, those twinkling eyes, that contagious laughter and that musical voice. She had been the apple of the eye of our entire family. She had been the brightest, the smartest, and the most talented—a daughter to my mother, a son to my father, a brother and sister to me. I always wondered how my tiny girl, my 5'2" Thumbelina, had done it all: so much more than I had ever managed to do, in so little time. She was a medal-winning athlete, an extraordinary orator, a fantastic dancer and always a top student. And now, she was dead. And it was my fault.

They all think so too; I know they do, though they don't say so to me. I see it in their hooded eyes; in the way Mom looks away when I speak to her; in the way that Papa's body becomes frigid when I hug him; in the way Bhaiyya looks at me, rage simmering underneath that too-calm look of his. I feel horribly guilty, so guilty that many a time I think life is no longer worth living, even though my doctor tells me that there is nothing I could have done about it. After all, I had no reason to believe that he would behave in that way; no reason to believe that this man, whom I had once thought of as gentle and kind, would be capable of this heinous, unimaginable crime.

I met Abhay at the gym. He was running on the treadmill; a grim, flat, unsmiling look on his face, as he increased his pace, going faster and faster, breathing harder and harder. I remember exactly how he looked then: fair skin, dark stubble, bright, fierce eyes that looked older than their years, the long floppy hair which he kept brushing away from his eyes. He was tall and well-built, his taut body spoke of hours at the gym. I'm not sure what prompted me to approach Abhay that day. Maybe it was because everyone else there was geriatric, or maybe it was because I was bored out of my mind with the repetitions that the trainer was making me do.

When he came to the cooler to get some water, I smiled at him, and put out my hand to shake as I introduced myself.

'Hi! I'm Aarti Singh.'

He looked uncomfortable, but I thought that maybe it was because he was breathless after the run.

'Abhay,' he said, looking down at the floor, quickly gulping down the water and then walking away.

I was surprised. After all, rarely did boys walk away from me. I do not claim to be Miss India or anything like that, but I had always had my way with boys, feeling more comfortable with them than with girls. The next day we met again, at the same water cooler. This time he seemed friendlier; he smiled, and we began talking. He was doing law from some small college in Uttar Pradesh; he said he did not attend classes but was learning on the job, helping his father with cases. I told him that I was a second year student at Delhi University, studying English. When I told him that he had a good body, he just looked away and blushed, the cat having got his tongue, as it often did when he was with me.

Abhay was not used to speaking to girls which, in my naiveté, I didn't realize till much later. That was my first mistake. I had assumed that Abhay, a member of a chic gym in a posh area, was like the rest of us. That he had grown up going to co-ed schools, talking to girls, studying and playing with them, and maybe even hooking up with them. It was only later that he told me that I was the first female friend he had ever had; that where he grew up, girls didn't speak to boys, not till they were married at least. It was a strange world, unknown to me. I knew it existed—we all knew—but I had been shielded from it, living as I did in my own little South Delhi cocoon. Maybe that is why I enjoyed speaking with him—out of a feeling of curiosity about a world I did not know; a world that was so close to me, yet so far away. Maybe I felt that I could bring him into my world, help him, and somehow alleviate the sorrow and pain that I saw in his eyes. Only now do I realize that Abhay was too far gone even before I met him. I blame myself for not seeing the signs that stared me in the face all along.

2 December 2008

I remember the day because it was the day after Kalpu's 16th birthday. I woke up with a terrible back pain, unable to go to college or to the gym. As advised by my doctor, I spent a day in bed, watching TV serials and movies, till I could no longer look at the screen. That is when Abhay called me; the poor guy seemed really worried.

'You never miss the gym, even on a Sunday!' he exclaimed, clearly distraught. The genuine solicitude in his voice was sweet; especially since none of my college friends had bothered to ask why I had missed college. I told him that it was just a pesky backache; I had probably overdone it at the gym.

'But nothing ever happens to you,' he said. I laughed at his concern. He was worse than my mother, but I was touched by it. Who would have thought that this forlorn, serious young man cared so much about me? I guess we were real friends. We did see each other every day, after all, and I had grown fond of him.

'Aarti, I'm worried about you,' he said, the pain apparent in his voice.

'Abhay, I'm fine. If you want, come over and see for yourself!'

'What do you mean?' he asked.

'I mean, come over after the gym. I'm only five minutes away.'

It seemed natural to invite him over. And, to be honest, I was bored and I wouldn't mind the company.

He seemed hesitant and puzzled at my invitation, but in the end he accepted. Only when he came over that first time, did it strike me that we were from two totally different worlds. For the first time I noticed his old shabby sneakers, his unfashionable track pants, his worn-out T-shirt, his falling-apart backpack. He took off his shoes outside my house; no one did that but the domestic help. He was uncomfortable in the living room and around the household staff that served him water. With me, he was formal and strange, and looked at me with an expression on his face that I hadn't seen before.

The image that I had of him from the gym—the handsome fit guy who ran the fastest and lifted the heaviest weights—vanished; and now I saw a young, vulnerable, uncomfortable young man who looked utterly and totally lost. But it was in this avatar of his that I became attracted to him. I had liked him as a friend, and I had enjoyed the attention he paid me, but seeing him there, on the sofa, nervously running his fingers through his hair, my heart began fluttering.

I tried my best to make him feel comfortable in my home. It wasn't all that opulent, not by Delhi standards at least. It was only outside in the small park where I suggested we go for a stroll that he became the Abhay I knew.

I don't know what prompted him to tell me about himself. Maybe it was the stark contrast between his own home and what he called my 'palace house', maybe it was his relief at getting out of it, or maybe because he saw me weak and vulnerable with my back pain. But he told me about his parents: his abusive, alcoholic father, and his mother who, till now, had always buckled under his father's bullying, but had finally decided to stand up to him. Abhay was proud of her newfound courage, but it made living at home unbearable. There was constant friction as his father thrashed his mother and his mother fought back, and then they just screamed at each other while his mother threatened to call the police.

On his twenty-first birthday, he had asked his father for a gym membership. His panacea for the torture at home was running and lifting, and he wanted a place to which he could escape. In an unusual, generous gesture, his parents had given him an expensive gym membership; and to make every rupee count, he made sure never to miss a day.

'Thank you,' he said, looking at me, his eyes shining like lanterns in the darkness of the park.

'Thank you for?' I asked, confused.

'For helping me. You...you bring some happiness into

my life, Aarti. If it weren't for you, I do not know how I would go on,' he said.

I was at a loss for words. I had never thought that my friendship meant so much to him. In the moment of silence that followed, I reached over and kissed him. I'm not sure why I did it. Perhaps it was because I felt lonely and weak, or perhaps it was just hormones.

I had kissed a few boys before, but I could tell that it was new for him. He sat there, stunned, his mouth open, before he returned it. I didn't regret kissing him; after all, he was nice and hot, and I felt bad for him—this lonely, vulnerable guy, who made me feel as if I were the most important girl in the world.

Things should have stopped there. I wanted them to, but I was weak and I used him for my own purposes. I had just been dumped by Rohan Mistry, whom I had liked for two years. I had been on cloud nine when he finally asked me out, only to dump me two weeks later. I wondered if I had done anything wrong. We had had several enjoyable dates. I had always looked my best, and I had tried not to be difficult with him at all. Maybe the problem was, that I had been too nice. Whatever it was, after fourteen days of sweet dating, Rohan had gone cold. He stopped replying to my WhatsApp messages, stopped answering my calls and responding to my Facebook messages; and then, one day, out of the blue, he sent me an email saying that he wanted to focus on his cricket at the moment, and couldn't handle the distraction of a girlfriend—'girlfriend, even as nice and hot as you', was the bone he threw me.

I was devastated. I had liked Rohan for such a long time; and exactly when I thought I had him, he had dumped me. It was an understandable blow, but I didn't realize that it would hurt me as much as it did.

So, then, Abhay was like a balm to my wounded vanity. I basked in the attention he gave me; in the sweet little things he did for me—hand-written notes, chocolates, and flowers—all the silly little old-fashioned things about which I'd only read in novels but which no guy had bothered to do for me. And the kissing never stopped, things only got more intense as Abhay became a more confident and better kisser.

All along, I was clear about one thing: Abhay was just my friend (I guess with benefits) and I *never* thought of him as my boyfriend. Though Abhay was undeniably handsome, he was different from us. He spoke in an uncouth way, dressed unfashionably, and behaved in a slightly ghatee way. I couldn't imagine what it would be like to introduce him to the world as my boyfriend—everyone would probably make fun of me. So I never invited him to my college parties, never took him out with my friends, never even told anyone that he was more than just a pal.

Things between us continued in this way for a while, and though I saw Abhay every day at the gym, and sometimes even after that, I couldn't forget Rohan, no matter how hard I tried. He had a new girlfriend now, some pretty bimbette from a private college, and while he was nice to me every time he met me at a party, I began to hate him, and I hated myself even more. It was on such a night, after I had seen Rohan making out with his arm candy that I called Abhay and we made love. Well, I'm not sure making love is the right term. It was more like I had sex, and he made love. I don't know what came over me; maybe it was because I was drunk (I don't usually have more than a peg, but that night I had had three) or maybe it was because of Rohan, or simply because I was home alone; but I ended up taking solace in Abhay. I'm ashamed to say that it was I who ultimately asked him to do it with me. It was an awkward messy affair. Although I had gone all the way a few times before, it was clearly the first time for Abhay; but somehow, we did it—I, fuelled by alcohol and he, fuelled by passion.

As we lay in my bed—his arm around me, my head on his chest—I was lost in deceitful thoughts, wondering what it would have been like if I had been lying on Rohan's chest instead of his. He told me that he loved me. He stroked my hair and said that I was the person whom he loved the most in the world, and he was grateful that I had come into his life. He told me, now on the brink of tears, his voice heavy with emotion, that I gave him the courage and the will to carry on living every day.

I had known that he felt deeply about me, but this, this was a little too intense for me. I cringed in silence and decided not to say anything at all.

Over the next few days, I decided to create a little distance between us. I told him I was busy with college work. I changed my gym timing and I stopped chatting with him on the phone. But that didn't stop him. One day after ten phone calls and twenty SMSs (this was the beginning of my experiencing his crazy side), he came over to my house unannounced. He was unshaven, ragged, with dark circles under his eyes; and he looked ill. He quivered as he spoke with me, asking me why I was behaving like this. He asked me, with almost childlike innocence, if it was because I didn't love him anymore.

Love him anymore? I had never loved him in the first place. But what could I say to him? To be honest, I felt scared. I was scared of the way his eyes were twitching, scared of his shaking hands, and his heaving chest. I didn't know what to say; my words were stuck in my throat. I told him with great difficulty and as gently as I possibly could that though he was my best friend, though I loved him dearly, it was simply as a friend, maybe even as a brother, but nothing more than that.

I didn't know whether he was sad, or happy, or angry; I could not tell from the strange blank expression on his face. But then he got up and left, without saying a word. And more than anything else, I was just relieved.

In the days that followed, he didn't do anything particularly crazy. He behaved mostly normally, so I felt comfortable going to the gym again, though I avoided late-night meetings. He didn't refer to our conversation nor did he act strangely; so I started believing that maybe that day had just been an aberration.

Life was steady and stable. I didn't know it, but it was the calm before the storm. I was doing well in college. I thought I had more or less gotten over Rohan, and there was even this other boy in whom I was mildly interested. But then shit hit the roof when Rohan, only 22-years-old, announced his engagement to the bimbette. I don't know what came over me, especially when I had been so sure that I was totally over him. I began having awful thoughts: why had he chosen her over me? Was there something wrong with me? Was I unattractive, ugly, fat, and ineligible? Why else would he have broken up with me after just two weeks of dating? It drove me crazy and, before I knew it, I did something I used to do rarely, but which I seemed to be doing more than I should: I got drunk with my girlfriends.

I made a few crucial mistakes that night. First, I got very drunk and dialled Rohan. Not once but twenty times. Second, when Rohan didn't respond, I called Abhay who, of course, immediately came over. I don't remember clearly what happened next. I think Abhay got really worried and tried putting me to sleep, or maybe he tried to make me eat something. We ended up sleeping together that night. I don't remember much, except for the look of blissful delight on Abhay's face.

The next morning I felt like crap. I didn't know what to do or how to feel. I was angry for breaking the promise to myself and for sleeping with Abhay again when I knew that he loved me, while I didn't love him back. As was to be expected, Abhay went crazy with his text messages and phone calls; first out of concern for me, and then out of fear and anger when I didn't respond to any of them. To tell the truth, I was afraid of him and his reactions—he could get so angry and intense. I decided once again to cut off all communication with Abhay, come what may.

Maybe it was destiny, maybe it was simply timing, but just after Rohan announced his wedding, Papa showed me Shiv's photograph. He was the son of one of Papa's college batch-mates, a man Papa admired and liked. He was settled in the US and was working in a software company in San Francisco. Though I privately thought that all engineers were dorks, in the photograph Shiv looked really handsome, even more handsome than Rohan. To be honest, he won hands down over Rohan on all fronts. He was better-looking, better-educated and also wealthier. Papa had sent my photographs to Shiv, who had apparently liked them. He wanted to come down to India to spend time with me so we could get to know each other. I don't know why I said yes; it's not as if I had any desire to get married. I mean, I hadn't even had a *proper* boyfriend yet. Before I knew it, Shiv landed in Delhi, at my doorstep, and within just a few days he won me over.

Shiv was kind, sweet and sophisticated, despite being an engineer. I was proud to have him by my side and I sensed a love from him that was softer, kinder and much less scarier than what I had experienced from Abhay. Shiv proposed to me within a week; it felt right to say yes to him and we were engaged to be married.

Life became a whirlwind of shopping for saris and jewellery, making wedding preparations and Skyping with Shiv whenever I was at home. In a way, this activity was good for me, because whenever I had a free moment, I would start thinking about my coming life in America and feel incredibly scared. And whenever I felt insecure, I desperately wanted to speak with Abhay. I realized then that I did love Abhay in some obscure way. It wasn't in the same way as I loved Shiv, but it was something true and real. I loved Abhay because I felt safe with him; I basked in the selflessness of his love. I couldn't say the same about Shiv, not at this moment at least. I respected Shiv, trusted his capabilities, knew he could take care of me. Did I love him? No, not really; but I was sure that I could learn to love him over time. So I kept myself busy. I had pretty much stopped going to college (Shiv and I had decided that I would take a transfer to a university in the US) and I no longer went to the gym. I avoided Abhay's phone calls, and just told him I was busy with studies and projects with little time to spare.

Then one day I ran into Abhay at my neighbourhood Café Coffee Day, where I often went to get away, read a book, relax. I was surprised to see him there; I wondered what he was doing so far away from his home (and world) and so close to mine. My guts told me that he was here to see me, but I had never taken Abhay for the stalker-variety so I quickly dismissed my thoughts.

It was an awkward interaction. I asked him what he was doing there. He told me casually that he had a meeting in the area and had come to grab a coffee since it was the only place he knew in the locality. I knew that he was lying. He never drank coffee; in fact he *hated* coffee. The only beverage that he ever drank was water. I accepted his explanation, though I knew that I should have suspected something, but he just seemed *so* normal to me then.

He asked me how I was doing in college, and joked that I had gained weight (which I had, since I had stopped going to the gym). I asked him how things were with him, and he said they were fine. He had started working part-time and he was enjoying it. Besides, it also kept him out of the house. When I asked him about the situation at home, I could see his face tense and darken as a shadow crossed over it. It was apparent that things weren't okay. I should have probably been there for him, as he would have been there for me. But I didn't know how or what to say to him.

And then suddenly he asked me, in the calmest, most casual fashion, 'You're not thinking of dating someone else, are you?'

Even though he was calm, there was a dark menacing undertone to his question and I felt inexplicably scared. I gave him an uncomfortable smile.

'Oh no, I'm just so busy with college. I couldn't even *think* about it.'

'Good!' he replied with a calm smile. 'You know, if you were with someone else, I would first hang him, and then hang you.'

And with that, he gave me a hug and left.

I was scared out of my wits, and I couldn't understand why. Of course I didn't believe that Abhay would kill me, or Shiv, but the way he had said it...it just didn't seem right. Before I could ponder over Abhay's threats, my mother summoned me. At any given point in time, there always seemed to be some sort of a wedding crisis to deal with.

Thinking back, it's not as if Kalpu had not known. I remember the evening vividly. Kalpu and I were trying on blouses, just brought back by the tailor, and she saw Abhay's name flash on my phone. He had gotten into the habit of calling and messaging me multiple times a day; a habit that I chose to ignore.

'Didi, how is Abhay? He used to come over so often. Why doesn't he anymore?'

'God knows,' I replied, trying to evade the topic. I just didn't want to think about the guy.

'Is he angry you are marrying Shiv Bhaiyya?'

'I don't know, Kalpu,' I said, a little exasperated. 'He's odd.'

'He seems like a nice guy. I ran into him at Café Coffee Day the other day.'

'Which one?' I asked, taken aback. Abhay at CCD, a second time?

'The one in our colony.'

'When was this?' I asked tensely.

'A few days ago. I was just meeting the wedding planner there.'

'Kalpu, stay away from him, okay? He's a freak.'

'Why Di? He seems like a nice guy. He bought me a coffee.'

'Kalpu,' I said sternly, getting her attention, 'the guy is a little odd and scary too. I don't know what's up with him. He calls me a hundred times, he thinks I'm his girlfriend, I feel like he stalks me too.'

'Does he know you are getting married?' she asked.

'No,' I said in a small voice, realizing more than ever before what a coward I was.

'Why don't you just tell him?' she asked me in a puzzled tone.

'It's not so simple, Kalpu; the guy loves me or something. I don't want to cause him any pain. Plus, I'm afraid he'll do something to himself or maybe even to me if he finds out.'

After a moment's silence, Kalpu said, 'Di, maybe you are overreacting. Just tell him. I'm sure he'll understand.'

'Maybe you're right.'

Little did we know how wrong Kalpu was!

I didn't hear from Abhay for a while. His phone calls and texts dwindled and instead he took to emails and Facebook, something that I could avoid more easily. Before I knew it, the marriage festivities had begun. Shiv's entire family and close to a hundred friends were visiting from the US and it was all a happy, nerve-racking blur. I didn't sleep for six nights and seven days. The days were filled with pujas, and the nights were a whirl with parties. I woke up in the morning to the make-up person, sat through many pujas, got introduced to an army of Shiv's friends and family, and then it would be time to get ready for the evening function.

Of my own wedding, all I remember in great detail is getting ready; the opulent, colourful glittery, heavy clothes I wore for each function; the gold and diamond jewellery that was placed around my neck; the large nose ring that my grandmother insisted I wear, which eventually led to a nose bleed.

I had no time, energy or inclination to think about anything, let alone Abhay who had gone totally silent (thank God!) over the past few days. My biggest fear (when I had the bandwidth to fear) was that Abhay would gatecrash the wedding and create a scene. Thankfully, nothing so dramatic happened and the wedding went off as smoothly as a wedding could possibly go.

Shiv and I flew almost immediately to the US. We flew back home less than twenty-four hours after we landed at JFK. He didn't tell me what had happened. He just stirred me out of a deep, jet-lagged sleep and told me that Kalpu was sick and we had to go back home, *immediately*. I was too tired and sleepy to comprehend fully what was going on, and I could never have even imagined that the tragedy to which I was going back was the result of my own actions.

We attended Kalpu's funeral the evening that we landed. I couldn't bear to look at her dead body, and when I finally did, I didn't recognize the features that had been distorted by the burns. I told my parents that I didn't think that this was her, that it was somebody else. My sister, I said, was still alive somewhere. They just listened to me through their tears.

The phone records show that Abhay had called the landline fifty-eight times trying to reach me before he murdered Kalpana. The household staff said that Abhay had come over and had asked for me. When they told him that I was in America, he had asked for Kalpu, who met him outside the gate. They had then gone for a walk, in the direction of CCD. The police found Kalpu's dead body in the park across CCD. Underneath the burns there were bruises, and the autopsy revealed three broken bones.

Ironically, they nabbed Abhay in the gym, the place where we had first met. He admitted almost immediately to his crime. He told them that Kalpu had lied to him about my marriage; that he had wanted to teach her a lesson for hurting him badly by telling him that I was married. He insisted that he hadn't been wrong in what he did, and he was glad that she was dead. Apparently, he told the police that I too would have been angry with Kalpu for lying to him.

They put Abhay into prison, where he killed himself that evening. The police told him that Kalpu had not been lying, that indeed I was married and had moved to the US. His cellmate said that Abhay had slit his wrists using a pen. He bled to death that night. He had scribbled, 'I am sorry, Kalpu,' on his arm. I don't know what he told the police, or what they told my family, but Abhay was never mentioned to me again.

Though my parents, the police and the doctors tried to convince me otherwise, I knew I was responsible for not just one, but two deaths; and I would have to live with this burden for the rest of my life.

೮

Heartbreak

Ever since I was a little girl, I have wanted and loved only one thing: dance. Sadly, it was also the one thing that my family looked down upon, nautanki they called it. Well...that isn't entirely true; my family did endorse one dance, and that was kathak—the introduction to dance for my sisters and me. It turned me off for a couple of years, but then I couldn't stay away for long from my passion. And somehow even against my family's disdain for all things dance and Bollywood, I found dance again, or maybe, it found me.

I was a natural. Not in the classical dance that they forced down our throats at school, but the Western dance forms—especially Bollywood—in which I excelled and where I was like a fish in water—swimmingly good.

How did it all start? A little bit of Shahid Kapoor, a lot of Hrithik Roshan and Shiamak Davar, and a whole lot of dancing by myself in the bathroom with my headphones on.

My parents' finding out was inevitable, and I awaited with dread the day on which they would. Would they stop my dancing forever? Would they take away my iPod? Ban my watching movies? I kept up my marks to the minimum standard, did all the things they wanted me to, like reading boring books and going to math tuitions; but while I was doing all this, there was always a tune playing in my head, a tapping in my toes, and a song on my lips. And then one day they saw me dance, and that changed everything.

I was fifteen. It was our annual school function, and I was the lead. I danced, my heart, feet and soul, all one with the music. They were shocked, and so was I by their reaction. My dancing spoke to them like my tongue never could, and within six months they sent me to Mumbai to join junior college and to join classes at Shiamak Davar's Dance Academy. They say dreams are just wild horses running around in our heads, but in my case my horses truly were dancing their way to reality.

It didn't take me long to get a hang of Mumbai. Everyone back home in Indore was worried about me. How would a 16-year-old manage? I was not, though, I knew that this was the city for me, this was the city that would teach me, use me, and one day set me free.

Shiamak Davar's Dance Academy

'Kanak baby, move faster, move those feet faster; you're the SLOWPOKE of the group. Step up, you're ruining the sequence!' scolded Masterji, our teacher and chief choreographer.

'Yes, sir,' I said in a whisper, out of breath, wiping the perspiration off my forehead, my eyes and mouth.

'Don't yes sir me, baby doll. JUST DO IT,' he said, with a thrust of his hips.

And then I screwed up again and again till finally I had to step out of the sequence. The group preferred to perform with an uneven number of dancers rather than have a loser like me with them.

Those were my days at the academy. I was the worst dancer in the school. Who could have ever imagined it? Sometimes, some of my sympathetic co-dancers (most were mean and competitive) reminded me that I was the youngest here by far, and also the newest, so I should go easy on myself. But these were all excuses. I was in Mumbai, living my dream, and I had to be the best. Right now, I was the worst dancer in the entire academy. I had never been so depressed in my life.

Along with the sour always comes the sweet; and one late summer night as I was practicing alone in an empty, stuffy, sweaty studio, I found Pranjal watching me practice; an amused look on his handsome face.

'You aren't too bad, yaar,' he said with a friendly smile. 'A little more work on the lateral movements and I think you could be really good.'

I didn't know how to respond to him. He stood there smiling at me. I took in his fitting black T-shirt, which showed off his sculpted body, the yellow bandana tied around his long hair.

'Uh, thanks,' I said awkwardly, not knowing how else to respond to him.

'Want to do a sequence together?' he asked.

'Uh, sure,' I said, wishing I had worn one of my cuter dance outfits. I was conscious of the fact that I was wearing my rattiest tights (you could even see the line of my underwear), a worn-out and faded T-shirt and that I was dancing barefoot, something that our teachers hated us doing; but that was how I had been dancing all my life.

I pulled down my T-shirt, hoping to cover my butt, and checked him out while he changed the music.

'Dirty dancing?'

'My favourite,' I responded with a smile.

I wasn't lying, it *was* my favourite; and while I didn't have Olivia Newton-John's blonde locks, I sure did have her moves. And that's how our love story began, not over a coffee date, nor over some cheesy movie, but over a perfect performance of dirty dancing.

With Pranjal's entry into my life, suddenly things looked brighter. He was an exceptional dancer, and at eighteen, he was one of the academy's youngest shining stars. He showed me the ropes, helped me with my moves, and shared academy secrets. I became less worried about being the best, or in my case, NOT being the worst, and I actually started enjoying my life. On Pranjal's advice I started attending college more regularly, and I even joined the college dance troupe where, as was to be expected, I was the best. This was a big boost to my confidence. I even made new friends in college—two nice guys, Ankur and Kaushal—who were surprisingly proficient dancers. Over hours of practice, the three of us became good friends, and I suggested that they audition for the academy; and much to my delight, they both got in.

Great dancing, good friends and the sweetest boyfriend, what more could a girl ask for? Just when life in Mumbai seemed to be perfect, things took an unexpected turn. Over the past few months, Ankur and I had become close. Pranjal had been offered a role as a back-up dancer in a Bollywood film and was always busy these days, out on some shoot or the other. I missed him, and to fill up that gap in my life, I turned to Ankur. Though he was an average dancer, he was tall (troupes love tall dancers), hard-working and utterly cooperative—qualities that few dancers had—and so he was doing well at the academy. Ankur gave me full credit for his success; he told me that I had inspired him to follow his passion, to join the academy and to take up dance seriously. Sometimes I felt a little guilty. After all, unlike most of us, Ankur was a good student, and he probably had a bright future in some multinational company somewhere. Despite all his hard work, the bitter truth was that he was only an average dancer and that no matter how much he tried, his future in the big bad world of dancing was limited, if not non-existent.

I clearly remember that day. It was an unusually lovely December evening. Ankur and I were taking a break from dancing, strolling on Juhu beach. We goofed around, gossiped a little about some of the neurotic characters in the academy and were generally having a good time when, awkwardly, like a stiff dancer trying to do a pirouette, he became serious.

'Kanak, I want to talk to you about something.'

I instantly had an uncomfortable feeling about this conversation.

He cleared his throat. 'You know, I've always admired you, from the minute I saw you in college. I think you had come straight from practice. You were wearing a leotard, tights, and leg warmers which made you look a little silly in the monsoon.' He spoke in a quiet voice, though there was a smile on his face.

'I didn't know that we would become such good friends, and I really didn't ever think that I would feel this way about you,' he continued.

'Which way?' I asked nervously, in a small voice, though it was a dumb question with only one obvious answer.

'I...I love you, Kanak,' he said, not looking into my eyes which I would expect a confident lover to do, as Pranjal always did with me.

We sat there for a few minutes; an awkward, pregnant silence between us.

'Ankur, you...you're like my brother. I care a lot for you, but you know that I love Pranjal. I've been in love with him for a while now, and he loves me too.'

He didn't respond to what I had said, but held his gaze steady, fixed on a spot between his knees.

'Ankur, you're my best friend. I don't want things to change between us,' I said mustering all the courage I had, though I had been terribly taken aback by his confession.

Ankur didn't say anything. He just nodded his head; and then we walked back together to the road, the laughter and lightness between us gone. I didn't speak to Ankur for the next few days. Several times I picked up my cell phone to send him a text, but I didn't know what to say. Thankfully, when I saw him a few days later at the academy, things between us seemed almost normal.

It was around this time that things between Pranjal and me started getting weird. Bollywood was taking a toll on him. He had started doing drugs occasionally with his new dance pals. He went out a lot to bars, was constantly tired and cranky, and got into terrible temper tantrums, especially with me. I tried to be understanding. I am sure he too would have had he been in my position, but it was incredibly difficult to deal with him all the time. I just couldn't figure out *what* would make him feel better. I felt like I had tried it all. I had even tried cooking for him in my small shabby PG kitchen after I read somewhere that food is the key to a man's heart. Pranjal did swallow whatever I had made for him, but it definitely did not put him into a better mood.

While I was up to my eyebrows in the quest for a solution to Pranjal, I made friends with some of the older girls from the academy. They were all very talented dancers but Masterji had once told me that he didn't think any of them had much of a future except as back-up dancers because they had neither the vigour nor the discipline to make it beyond that. Though they spoke only about three things—Bollywood, boys and sex—I really enjoyed their light-hearted and frivolous banter. Especially after the weirdness and tension with Ankur and Pranjal over the past few weeks, it was nice taking a break from the boys and hanging out with girls.

I became especially close to Pinky—a short vivacious girl, who was always the life of the party. She wasn't particularly nice-looking, so she didn't have much of a future other than as choreographer (so said Masterji) but she was an incredibly good dancer with an attitude to match. She could put any dance floor on fire. Despite her lack of looks, Pinky seemed to have a number of men in her life. After practice, one or the other of them always came to pick her up on his motorbike (sometimes a car, which got her excited). She seemed unable to hold on to a man, though.

'Kanak baby, you and Pranjal must be having wild sex, yaar. You've managed to hold on to him for so long!' she exclaimed one day as we went for some coffee after practice.

I wasn't sure how to admit to Pinky that I was a virgin, and that Pranjal and I had never had sex.

'You must be doing it at least once a day, maybe twice, na?' she said jokingly.

'No, nothing like that,' I said shyly, blushing a little over talking so openly about my sex life.

'Why are you blushing like a virgin? You guys DO do it, na?' she asked.

'Well...'

'Don't tell me you're a virgin!'

'Kind of...' I admitted.

'Shiiitt, Kanak. You're mad! You'll lose him if you don't *do* it with him.'

'What do you mean?' I asked her. What she had said wouldn't have meant anything to me earlier; but after

Pranjal's recent behaviour, I had indeed been getting a little concerned that something in our relationship wasn't right.

'Men are like dogs, baby. If they don't get it, they become cranky. They need it. It's very weird. It's not like us women at all. We like to talk, jabber, share our feelings, hold hands. Men, they need to have sex.'

I didn't respond to her, only absorbed what she had said. But after I left, I seriously wondered if it was time for Pranjal and me to move to the next level in our relationship.

The next step happened sooner than I had planned. A few days after my conversation with Pinky, Pranjal told me that he was going to Lonavala to participate in a dance contest. He wanted me to dance with him, not as a partner—it was a solo dance competition—but in a short cameo that was part of his performance. I was thrilled. Masterji wanted me to start competing from the following year, but this would give me some exposure. Besides, there was that other thing. I was a little young, I had just turned seventeen but, according to Pinky, everyone in Mumbai was doing it at fifteen these days, so it didn't seem like it was a big deal. Plus, I could feel that gaping hole in our relationship growing bigger. Maybe sex was indeed the solution.

We were in Lonavala for a week, though ours was only a ten-minute performance. Pranjal was in a great mood; he was pretty confident of winning the competition. We had seen the other dancers perform, and we were light years ahead of them. We spent a lot of time together and made love for the first time. It wasn't as easy as I had thought it would be. For one thing, it was *very* painful, much more painful than it had seemed on the internet. Moreover, Pranjal wasn't very experienced. He wasn't a virgin like I was, but he had only done it a few times before; so he was nervous, almost as nervous as I was. Also, we couldn't do it in one go. It was too painful for me, and he couldn't really manage to get the angle right. All in all, having sex for the first time was neither romantic, nor was it fun or pleasurable. But we kept at it and, finally, after a few nights of failure, he was able to get his 'thing' inside me, and we technically made love. As we did it more often it got easier and even enjoyable. I realized a few things about sex. It is much easier for boys than for girls, and it is also instant gratification for them. For girls, it takes some getting used to, and it is only after a lot of it, that it becomes fun.

Having sex with Pranjal did improve our relationship. It definitely became more exciting, and it felt like we had sort of moved on to the next step in our romance. However, while I felt more closely connected to him, I also felt more vulnerable and insecure. Pinky thought I was being silly; but I felt as if I had given him something special, something that a girl should give only to one guy in her life. Instead of feeling closer to him and more loved, I felt guilty and scared. Maybe it was just the mindset that well-brought-up Indian girls don't have sex before marriage. Maybe I knew deep down inside me that Pranjal and I would break up some day, and that it would hurt me really badly.

Some things come to an end, others begin. The competition wasn't special only because we had made love for the first time, it was also because Pranjal won his first major dance competition. After that, his career took off in a big way. I too got several Bollywood offers, some of which I took and others which I did not. Unlike Pranjal, who was a natural dancer, I knew that I had to work hard on my technique before I could join the big league. The more well-known Pranjal became, the bigger the gap grew between us. We continued to have sex, but in many ways, it was like a tape holding together a broken relationship. Eventually, the tape lost its glue and the relationship broke down. We did not sit down and have a chat about our break-up; we just stopped laughing, dancing, having fun, until we even stopped talking. I would see him at the academy and we would exchange pleasantries, but it wasn't long before he left it. After all, he was the best dancer there; maybe even better than Masterji, and there wasn't much more that he could learn in this place.

I didn't want to become one of the typical girls in my college who, after break-ups with their boyfriends, cried their eyes out and moped. That wasn't me—it would never be—but nor did I quite know how to deal with this. I told myself that, after all, I was only seventeen, I hadn't expected anything permanent from this relationship, I had not been expecting to *marry* Pranjal. But still, I had loved him, I *still* loved him, and it hurt that he was no longer in my life. For so long, Pranjal had given me so much happiness, and now that it was taken away for me, I felt sad, lonely and unloved.

To make myself feel better, I spent a lot more time with Ankur and Kaushal. The three of us had decided to do a dance for our annual college function. My break-up had in some way unhinged me, and the thought of putting up a scintillating dance performance at the function helped anchor me a bit.

I hadn't planned to tell Ankur about my break-up with Pranjal because I didn't want him to get any ideas about me. But I spent so much time with him that it was difficult to hide anything, and I ended up telling him. I still had many bitter, blue moments, feeling low just when I thought I was beginning to get over it. Ankur would always ask me what was wrong, and one day, during a long walk on Marine Drive, I told him what had happened between Pranjal and me.

'That idiot!' muttered Ankur angrily, as I finished narrating the story to him.

'Why is he an idiot? I guess some relationships just don't work out,' I said, trying to sound cheerful, though the reality was that even telling him had brought me on the verge of tears.

'It's just not right for him to make love to you and then to break up without any reason at all.'

'There *was* a reason, Ankur.'

'Accha? What was it?'

I didn't have an answer to that. The truth was that there had been no reason. It was not as if anything bad had happened between us, or that I had wronged him, or he had wronged me. It was just that our relationship had fallen apart.

'We drifted apart.'

'That is *no* reason to break up. If you love someone, and if you say you love someone, then feelings just don't change like that. Not overnight at least!'

'I don't know. What you say sounds reasonable, but it doesn't really work that way. In real life, relationships fall apart, sometimes for no reason at all.'

'At least, that's what Pinky says,' I added.

Ankur smiled grimly.

'You're taking relationship advice from Pinky? She changes men as often as she changes sweaty leotards.'

'Ankur!' I said, with a little smile.

'I'm serious, Gargi. You're a special girl, and no man can treat you like this. I'm going to teach that ass a lesson.'

'What lesson?'

'A dance lesson.'

'What! He's a damn good dancer.'

'I'm KIDDING, Gargi, I'm not going to teach him anything related to dance. This...this is going to be a naach of a different sort,' he said, gazing into the distance with a contemplative but odd look on his face.

I should have said something to Ankur then, but the truth is that I liked the idea of Pranjal getting a beating from my friends. Deep down, I was very angry with him—angry for breaking up, angry for breaking my heart, angry for giving me something so good and then cruelly snatching it away. So, in what was to be the biggest mistake of my life, instead of stopping Ankur, I wrapped my arm around him, drew him close and kissed him on the cheek.

I didn't believe the news when I heard it. The corridors of the academy were abuzz with rumours, and a concerned Pinky broke the news to me: Pranjal had been the victim of an acid attack. In the state of shock that I was in after hearing the news, it didn't strike me that Ankur might have done this. I had all but forgotten our talk; and Ankur had just planned to jerk Pranjal around for a bit of fun, not ruin his entire life by disfiguring him.

But then I got an SMS from Ankur.

Job done. He will never get another girl in his life.

I called him right away.

'Ankur, what have you done?'

'Just made sure he never makes a fool of another girl again.'

'You...you...attacked him with acid?'

'Kaushal and I thought this was the best way,' he said grimly.

'Will he be okay?' I asked. I didn't know much about acid attacks, but I knew they were awful, irreversible and that they ruined people's lives; but surely, this couldn't have been so bad.

'He'll dance for the rest of his life, but with a mask on,' said Ankur with a mean laugh.

'I...I...can't believe this,' I said in a whisper, truly unable to take in what had happened.

'Isn't this what you wanted?' he asked, taken aback by

my reaction.

'Nooo,' I whimpered, breaking into a sob. 'I...I thought you were just going to push him around a bit, but this...No, I did not want you to go to this extreme, Ankur. I never dreamt you would,' I said, tears running down my face.

'Anyway, what has happened, happened for the best,' said Ankur breezily. 'Now that that asshole is out of the picture, you and I can be together. And I promise you that I'll *never* leave you.'

'You don't understand,' I whispered. I felt as if I were in an awful nightmare, from which I would wake up in Pranjal's arms any second.

'What don't I understand?' he said sharply.

'I...I love him, Ankur. I love Pranjal, I always have and I always will,' I said softly.

'Just because you've slept with him, doesn't mean that you have to be with him, Gargi,' said Ankur harshly. 'You and I are *meant* to be together, don't you get it?'

'It has nothing to do with that, nothing at all. I love him,' I said and then I hung up the phone. There was nothing else that I could, or wanted to, say to him.

I knew that I would get into trouble. I knew that Ankur and Kaushal would try to blame it all on me, but I knew I had to do it. I told the police the entire story, from start to finish, including the conversation I had had with Ankur on Marine Drive when he had threatened to teach Pranjal a lesson. I went to visit Pranjal at the hospital. I didn't recognize the mummy that I saw, bandages covering his face and lips. The acid had got his tongue too, and he couldn't speak coherently. He was only semi-conscious, and didn't know yet what had happened to him or even that he had been attacked. I didn't have the heart to tell him that I was the reason for his pain, the reason for his never being able to perform again, the reason for ruining his life. When I held his hand, whispering gently in his ear that it was me, I saw a tear roll down his eyes.

His words were garbled because of his injured tongue, but I caught the gist of what he was trying to say.

'Will I still be able to dance?' he asked.

'Yes,' I told him with all my heart. 'No one can ever take that away from you.'

I stayed that night with him in the hospital, until they took me away to jail. I dreamt of him and me dancing together at the academy, on the stage, on a movie screen. He was whirling me, twirling me, lifting me, and then he dropped me; but before I could hit the ground, he caught me and we were dancing gloriously again.

☙

My Sweet Sixteen

The day that Amit stopped calling me 'a fat cow', I should have guessed that something was wrong. After all, he had been taunting me for five years straight, from the very first minute he laid his eyes on me at our school gates. That he should stop for no particular reason at all should have made me wonder, but I was just very happy and relieved that the torture had finally stopped. Actually, it felt odd not to walk down the corridors of my school, scared, knowing that any second that brute Amit might crawl out of the woodwork and come after me. Yes, I was overweight; the fattest person in my grade, maybe even in my school, and though I had been desperately trying to lose weight (for many years now), I had not been lucky. There were a few good reasons for it, too. First, Amit's jeering did not help me; the more stressed I became, the more I ate. Eating was a stress buster for me, so it was sort of like the more he teased me the more weight I gained. All his insults had resulted in turning me into some sort of a social pariah, and I had only one friend, Molly. I was continually in a deep, dark hole where my only solace was food. Besides, in my family, *everyone* was fat. In fact I was the least fat of them all. We were from the heartland of Punjab, and eating is what my family lived for. My mother's sole self-appointed function in life was to cook for us and to feed us; and I sometimes felt that my dad worked hard only to put butter chicken on the table every night. No one in my family thought that my weight was off-putting or unattractive; and when I tried to diet, they always chastised me saying I was silly to try to reduce my weight.

I quickly adjusted to the taunt-free life. I began to walk a little more confidently down the passage, my self-esteem rose slowly out of the pits. I no longer felt bad about going to school every morning.

A week after he stopped sniping at me, a most surprising thing happened. Amit walked up to me, *smiled*, and said hello. I was so shocked that I didn't know what to say to him. All I could do was look at him uncomfortably. My first instinct was to feel nervous; what was he going to say to me now?

'What's up, Prachi?' he asked.

I wondered whether he was mocking me, and I waited for him to say something mean; but when he didn't, I clutched my books to my chest as if they were a shield, and said in a small, embarrassed voice.

'Uh, nothing,'

'I wonder whether you would like to have coffee with me sometime.'

I was stunned into silence. I just looked at him like a

daft cow, the very epithet he had thrown at me for years.

'I take that as a yes,' he said with a grin. 'Can I have your number? I'll WhatsApp you, and we can set it up,' he said.

'Uh...Sure.'

I gave him my number. I really had no choice in the matter. I was terrified of Amit Shah; he was the most popular guy in our school, basketball captain, athletics captain, prize-winning debater and a star bully. Who was I to say no to him? I was just a fat nobody about whom no one cared.

∽

'Amit Shah asked for your *number*?' squealed Molly, my best (and only friend), on the phone. 'What do you think he's going to do with it? I hope nothing bad,' she said, now concerned.

'He...uh...asked me out for coffee.'

'No way,' she said in utter disbelief. 'Amit Shah, hot stuff on campus, asked *you* out on a date? I simply don't believe it.'

Suddenly, I felt a little more than angry, especially since it was Molly saying it. What *was* the big deal? I wasn't so horrible, was I? After all, I did have nice hair and good skin; was it so unbelievable that a guy should ask me out on a date? It seemed to me that maybe Molly was jealous; after all, she had never been asked out before.

'What's the matter, Molly? Can't a guy ask me out on a date? I may be fat, but I'm not *so* bad either, you know.'

'Nothing like that, Prachi,' she said apologetically. 'Of course anyone can ask you out. You're a lovely person; but all I am saying is that it's strange that this guy is suddenly asking you out after years of picking on you.'

'It's not *that* strange, Molly, sometimes people change their minds, you know. Also I read somewhere that guys sometimes tease the girls they like before asking them out. Anyway, I'll talk to you later,' I said, a little annoyed by Molly's reaction. Maybe I should change my mind about being best friends with *Molly*, I thought to myself.

I didn't hear from Amit for a few days, but the very fact that he had stopped getting at me and had asked for my number made me decide to lose some weight. I was *done* with being fat, even if my family was not. I was done with hiding underneath salwar-kameezes and baggy clothes. I wanted to wear jeans and tight tops and maybe, one day, even a mini-skirt. I started eating less, and made it a point to go walking in the park. Just when I had lost hope, Amit WhatsApped me.

Amit: Hey, Prachi, what's up?

I felt more confident on WhatsApp with him than in person.

Prachi: Hey, yourself! Not much, and you?

Amit: Just got home from practice.

Prachi: Nice!

Amit: Do you have any hobbies? :)

Prachi: Yes. Reading, writing, singing...

Amit: I would love to hear you sing. I'm sure you sing sweetly.

Was this guy flirting with me? Was it possible?

Prachi: Thanks! I do sing pretty well.

Amit: I was wondering whether you were up for that coffee date?

Prachi: Yeah, sure.

Amit: How about Café Coffee Day tomorrow, 5 o'clock? I'll come straight from practice.

Prachi: Okie dokie :)

I couldn't believe I had a date with a guy, and that too with Amit. I wanted to enjoy this attention and this feeling, as no guy had ever given me more than a summing-up look. However, every time I remembered his former sneering and taunting, I felt really uncomfortable. In many ways I disliked him deeply, but then again nobody had ever asked me out on a date before. If only our memories were like SMSs that you could delete with the click of a button!

I was in a frenzy about what to wear on my date, and I settled on a black kurta with sequins, black tights and subtle gold earrings. I even went to the parlour to get my hair blow-dried. After all, my hair was my best asset.

Our date was a little awkward, mostly because of me. While I was pretty confident on WhatsApp, real life was a different story. I couldn't even look at him, let alone have a proper conversation with him. He finished his coffee pretty quickly, while I didn't even touch mine. On our way out, he touched my arm. I immediately turned peony pink; no guy had ever touched me before.

'Why are you so shy, Prachi?' he asked me softly, looking me in the eye. 'I know you may think I'm a demon, because

I have troubled you so much, but I'm not. I'm really sorry for all that.'

He looked genuinely ashamed and, with this apology, he turned around and left.

I was frozen to the spot watching him walk away. For the first time, I noticed his looks. He was handsome, tall and super-fit, with long flowing hair, and a confidence in his gait which I would never ever have.

His apology had touched my heart. Maybe, just maybe, Amit Shah was a nice guy after all.

Over the weeks that followed our first date, Amit and I grew friendlier. He was nice to me in school, he was always in touch on WhatsApp and we often met for coffee. As I lost more weight and as Amit and I became better friends, I grew more confident and our dates were more enjoyable. I had never understood it earlier, but I knew now why girls loved to have boys in their lives. It was such a fantastic feeling—exhilarating, uplifting, and dreamy all at the same time. I felt as if I were living on a cloud, looking down at that dark hole in which I had been buried for so long.

Molly, though, was not as happy as I was. She constantly warned me about Amit, reminding me of all the years during which he had teased me.

'Remember that time he pasted a picture of a cow on your locker? Remember that time when he made the whole class moo when you entered? I hope you don't forget all this when you are WhatsApping him all night long.'

'He's changed, Molly. He apologized for all that. He

said that he really liked me...he even said that he finds me pretty.'

'You *are* pretty, Prachi, no doubt; but Amit...I'm not sure about him. He just doesn't seem like a nice guy.'

I took Molly's concern as jealousy. She didn't have a hot guy like Amit chasing her, did she? In fact, she had *no* guys chasing her at all. Of course, all this must have been hard for her. I decided to be a bigger person and to be kind to her, disregarding her misplaced advice.

Amit officially became my boyfriend the day he kissed me (in my mind, at least). He was dropping me home on his bike, after an ice cream and, without warning, he pulled into a quiet lane beside my house, turned around and kissed me gently on my lips. I almost fell off the bike in surprise. He continued to kiss me and then, though I had never kissed before and had no idea how to, I tried to recall what I had seen in movies, and returned his kiss.

It was the most romantic moment of my life. That kiss opened up something within me—I think it was desire. I started to think of him all the time; during school, while I was doing my homework, during my singing lessons and even when I went to sleep. It was the best feeling that I had ever had, and I figured that *this* was love. The following week, when Amit asked me to come over to his house, I immediately said yes, hoping for and desperately wanting more kisses from him.

I couldn't control myself physically with Amit: the more he kissed me and touched me, the more I wanted him. When he touched me in places which I never imagined that he would, I didn't stop him, because his touch was electric, it felt so good. Pretty soon, Amit and I were meeting at his place almost every other day, and we were doing more and more, physically. The further we went, the more I wanted; though something inside me told me to be careful, it was difficult when we were in the heat of the moment. Above all, I was in love with Amit and I wanted to please him. If I tried to stop him, he would whine, and in a childish voice say, 'Baby, please don't stop me.' And when he spoke like that, I simply could not say no to him.

Once I started going over to his place, our coffee dates and late-night phone calls stopped. I should have noticed then that something was amiss, but I was so infatuated with Amit that I couldn't think clearly. Molly as usual tried to warn me.

'You know, Prachi, guys want only one thing. Make sure you take it slow. Guys just use and throw aside girls. Once they get what they want, they leave them.'

My Amit couldn't possibly be like that, I thought to myself. I figured that Molly was becoming greener with jealousy. As Amit and I got closer and closer, it became inevitable that we should start having sex. It's not that he forced himself upon me, not the first time at least. Even though I would like to, I can't blame him entirely for what happened, because the harsh reality—that I realize only now—is that a girl has to be responsible for her own body. There is no other way. I had never taken care of my body, and when it came to sex, I abused it, as I had done my entire life. Though I knew that it wasn't sensible, I let him have sex with me without using a condom. He said he loved me so much that he didn't want to use one. I believed him. Besides, I didn't know any better. At that point, I knew nothing about sex except what I had seen online. In school, they didn't teach us much about sex; our sex education course had consisted of a teacher who hesitatingly explained the male and female reproductive systems to us. I don't think she ever used the words 'penis' or 'vagina', and certainly not 'condom'. I had never seen a condom in my life, and I didn't know where to get one (and even if I had known, I probably would have been too embarrassed to buy one). I should have known better. I should never have had sex with Amit, at least not till I was prepared—mentally, emotionally and physically—and till I knew a little bit about how to care for my body. But he wanted it, and I didn't know how to say no.

It's not that I didn't enjoy getting physical with him. After the initial pain of the first few times, I did start enjoying it; but in some way it felt wrong to me. I had always thought that sex was about love, after all, wasn't it called 'making love'? But with Amit, it didn't feel as if any love was involved on his part, though I think that I loved him. When I missed my period, I didn't think much of it. Periods were a big headache in general, and I was always annoyed when I got them. There were a few other odd symptoms—painful nipples, swollen breasts, loss of appetite, a tiny bit of nausea—that I just ignored. And then I missed my period the following month too, and the symptoms got worse.

I got worried, and I wondered what was happening to me. It was Molly who suggested that I see her cousin who was a gynaecologist and who had a clinic close to my place. I had never consulted a gynaecologist, and I wasn't too keen on it. Molly and I argued. I told her that all this was probably due to the fact that, for the first time in my life, I was on a successful weight loss mission. The internet did say that when women lost a significant amount of weight, their periods were likely to get affected. But Molly insisted, so I went.

I wanted very badly to tell Amit but I just couldn't get myself to talk to him about it. We had been talking less and less those days because he was so busy, and I didn't want the few conversations that we had to be unpleasant. So, I decided to say nothing.

Dr Anju, Molly's cousin, was kind, pleasant and young, and I felt comfortable talking to her. She didn't seem judgemental or mean, and she told me that everything between us would be confidential. If I was worried lest she tell Molly, I should not be. I considered hiding the fact that I had been having sex with Amit, but when I told her of my symptoms, some of the first questions she asked me, were:

'Do you have a boyfriend?'

'Do you have sexual relations?'

'Have you had sexual intercourse and penetration with him?'

So I told her everything, about loving Amit, about having sex with him.

'Do you use a condom?' she asked me and I said, 'No,' not thinking much about it till I saw the concern in her eyes and a shadow across her face.

She took a urine sample and did a physical check. Then she broke the news to me as gently as she could. But a bomb is a bomb no matter how softly it lands on the earth.

'Prachi, I'm pretty sure you are pregnant. I'm doing another test just to confirm; but the initial results say that you are. I'm really sorry about this,' she said.

I almost fainted. 'Pregnant?' I whispered. 'Like...having a baby?'

'I'm afraid so, Prachi. I really wish you had used a condom. At your age, if you have frequent sex without a condom, pregnancy can take place very quickly.'

I sat there in silence for a while. Dr Anju reached out to hold my hand. 'You have options, you know,' she said. 'There are many ways to have an abortion. At your stage a surgery is probably the safest, but there are pills as well.'

'What will I tell my parents?' I said, thinking first of them and their reaction. They would be so unhappy with me! They'd probably throw me out of the house or maybe send me away somewhere. I knew that having the baby just wasn't an option. 'What am I going to do?' I asked Dr Anju before the tears started streaming down my face.

Dr Anju gave me the pills, and warned me that I had to take them immediately, else they would be harmful, and that they may not even work. Though I knew that I should take them, I could not get myself to do it. I couldn't get myself to do anything. I just fell deeper into that dark hole which I had thought I had left far behind. I started eating like it was no one's business, cloaking my sadness by eating large quantities of junk food. I was too afraid to tell Amit. What would I tell him? What would he say? The last thing that I wanted was for Amit to leave me.

As the days passed, I felt more and more confused. It was too late to take the pills. But I had bought two extra doses of what the doctor had prescribed, and I figured that I could probably take a triple-strength dose. Molly was the only one who knew about my pregnancy, and it was she who finally pulled me out of the hole and got me to take action. She wanted me to tell my mother, tell Amit and then figure out the next steps.

I was so nervous before telling Mom that when I sat down to talk to her, I just burst out into tears. She was surprised because I do not cry very easily. I slowly explained everything to her, leaving out no details. I had told myself that I had to be totally honest. I couldn't tell her half-truths and then get into further complications.

'I'm so sorry,' I said, weeping on her shoulder.

Some unfortunate stories have a silver lining, and for me, my mother was my silver lining. I had not known how she would react, but her gentle acceptance of my story was a pleasant surprise. She told me that I had done wrong, but that she understood and forgave me. With tears in her eyes, she said that she too was probably partly to blame for the way I had behaved. She told me that we would take care of it together; that she would be by my side.

'Don't worry,' she said. 'I won't tell Papa or your

brothers. This will be our secret for the rest of our lives.'

The conversation with Mom cheered me up and gave me the courage to speak to Amit. I met him at our usual coffee shop. He looked tired, worn out and had an angry scowl on his face. At that moment he looked like a demon, and I immediately felt scared. I wondered how I could have ever loved a guy like him.

At first, he had a look of disbelief plastered on his face; but within seconds his features were distorted into a cruel smile. 'It's probably someone else's, not mine. Who knows with whom else you have been sleeping!'

I couldn't bear his harsh words, and though I had promised myself that I wouldn't cry, the tears just came; and as soon as I started crying, Amit got up and left. I didn't want to go to school the next day, but Mom said that I should. She told me that I didn't have to be afraid of Amit. She said that we would deal with this in our own way, and that we would make sure that he paid for his behaviour.

I entered the corridor and was almost immediately surrounded by Amit's gang.

'Moooooo!' said one. 'Here comes the fat cow. This time, a fat, PREGNANT cow.'

I didn't know how to react. I couldn't believe that Amit would have been so cruel as to tell his friends.

'She's a slutty cow,' said another guy. 'I wonder if she'll give ME a little action,' he said, reaching out and pulling my plait.

I pushed my way past them, and walked away from

them as quickly as I could, almost running to the girls' bathroom. All the pills were in my backpack, and in my fit of rage, sadness and anxiety, I took out all twelve pills, three times the normal strength and swallowed them all. What had I done to deserve all this? Why was I being punished in this awful way? I didn't want to be pregnant. I didn't want to deal with this. In my agony, I beat my stomach as hard as I possibly could. I was going to kill this baby instead of me, this baby that had given me so much pain. I don't know when I fainted, or how much time I spent in that cubicle. All I know is that I woke up in a hospital bed.

Molly

I felt guilty and responsible for Prachi's disappearance. I was her best friend and the only one who had known about her problem from the very start. We found her unconscious in the girls' toilet, awash in her own blood. She was admitted to the ICU, and I was by her side for as long as her parents allowed me. The pills had done their work, and then more. She had aborted, but had also injured her uterus, and had to have a full hysterectomy. That meant that Prachi would never be able to have children.

Her parents asked me to leave, and every time I came back to see her in the hospital, they would not allow it, saying that Prachi was asleep, or that guests weren't allowed.

I tried again after a few weeks, but she had been discharged. Prachi's phone had been disconnected, her

Facebook account had been deactivated. Even her emails stopped. When I went over to her house, her parents looked at me like I were a stranger and told me that I was not welcome in their house. When I asked about Prachi, they told me that she no longer lived there and then slammed the door in my face. I asked around—her brothers, her cousins, the school authorities—but no knew or seemed to know where Prachi had gone. Prachi, my dear friend, had simply disappeared.

ℭ

Revenge

Mandeep

When I was a little boy, my father would ask me sometimes to come sit on his lap. I imagine that most kids would think back to such moments fondly, but when I remember, even now, I go rigid with fear. I would sit on my father's lap as still as possible, on the verge of tears, because I knew that, any second, a beating would come my way. I never knew what would trigger it off—it just depended on his mood or what he was watching on TV. If he got bored with it he would slap me, just like that, for no reason at all, sometimes so hard that my nose would bleed all over my shirt. I would be too scared to make a sound, because that would bring on another beating. So I would sit there, still as a shadow, till either my quivering mother came to get me, or till he threw me off because I was bleeding all over him.

It hadn't always been this way with us. There were

happier days when I was young: he would hold me, laugh with me, bring me small toys (all of which I threw away in anger when the beatings first started), and be what I guessed a father should be. I don't recall exactly when, but things starting changing. Though Ma has never told me the facts, she hints at problems with Papa's work. His factory burnt down, his employees screwed him, he lost all his savings, and then he had to send his family, us, away to my mother's place. We stayed with Nana and Nani for two years. What I remember most from those two years—more than anything else—was missing my father. I cried for him every night till, after a few months, I forgot about him, as kids tend to do. During those two years, he never came to visit us, not even once, and then suddenly he showed up one day—thinner, darker, more worn out, with thin grey hair—only a shadow of what I remembered of him. He didn't hug me or even touch me, and I recall being scared of him, nothing else. I hid behind my mother's sari pallu and the first thing that my father said to me with a sneer was, 'He's became a pansy, Mumma's boy, hasn't he?'

The beatings started shortly after we came home, occasionally at first and then more often. At first, Ma would intervene but then he would beat her up too, so, while he was beating me, she would lock herself in her room and cry. Slowly, like me, she became immune to the whole affair. The beatings continued, and while I didn't fear them as much as I once used to—resigning myself to them as a daily part of my day, like brushing my teeth, or combing my hair—I hated them more with each and every slap.

Arun

If I had wanted to, I could have beaten him up in a second. I was bigger, stronger, and faster. However, despite his diminutive size, when Mandeep came near me, I don't know why, but I wilted; and the strength that I had spent so long at the gym trying to build up, oozed out of me. There were many times when I wanted to clobber him badly—and I could easily have—but then, something would come over me and I would allow him to taunt me, jeer at me, throw things at me and, worst of all, steal my money. This had become somewhat of a daily routine. He would waylay me on my way back home from the gym and then demand my wallet. If I refused, he would at first verbally abuse me and then threaten to beat me. In the end, just to get rid of him, I would always hand over whatever I had.

One day, things changed and the seeds of revenge were sown. It was a hot day, so hot that the heat of the tarmac road seeped through my shoes to the soles of my feet. I was walking home after a rigorous workout, and all I wanted was to get myself a cool drink as soon as I could. Mandeep hadn't been bothering me for the past few days, and though I dreaded running into him, I thought that the heat would prevent him from roaming around. Just when a shop was in sight, and I could practically taste an ice cold Mirinda, I saw him, perched on his bike, thin as a reed, smiling that evil smile of his. The sight of him made me cringe, and I stopped, but only for a second—it was too hot to stand still. There was no going back now;

he had seen me, and I hastened my steps so that I could quickly pass him.

'Where are you going, Munna?' he jeered.

'Just home,' I said quickly, without stopping, looking at the road in front of me.

'You must pay me before you pass. Think of it as a toll.'

'I don't have anything on me,' I lied, feeling the rupee notes that my mother had given me, safe in my pocket.

'I don't think that's true,' he said in a silky tone. 'You know what happens to people who don't pay toll. They pay for it with their lives.'

With a smile he took a small, sharp knife out of his pocket and held it out for me to see before putting it back. And then, in a harder tone, 'Pay up, or it's the knife.'

I was sure that someone as vicious as Mandeep would not hesitate to use a knife. So, without a fight, I handed over my money to him. With a grin, he took the money from me, kissed it, placed it in his pocket and walked over to the small shop on the other side of the street. He bought two cold Mirindas and a packet of milk—and then he pinched the packet of milk with his finger making a hole in it, and threw it at me as if it were a water balloon.

I stood there watching my shirt get soaked in milk, as he walked away from me, laughing between his filthy teeth.

Roshni

'Who is the FATTEST of them all?' he yelled and I turned away. I was used to it by now, and though I hated him, hated him with every cell in my body, there was nothing that I could do except ignore him and walk away. Mandeep was the most awful, terrible, disgusting boy in our school, and *everyone* was scared of him. I don't know why but though he was short, skinny, and not very strong, he was the school's biggest bully. To my bad luck, one day, he picked on me and from thereon, made my life a living hell. During the first few months, I just cried every day, and used every excuse under the sun to skip school. But then I found courage to face him, and it came in the form of love. Arun and I were as different as chalk and cheese: he was fit, I was fat; he hadn't read a book in all his life, and my life revolved around books; I was at the top of the class, he landed up consistently at the bottom. Yet somehow, I really liked him. He was sweet and gentle, ever-smiling and always nice to me, which felt especially good after Mandeep's taunts.

One day, after school, he shyly asked me whether I would like some ice cream, and I happily agreed. It was our first real date—at least I thought of it as such. He bought chocobars for both of us, and as we walked together towards my bus stop, I saw Mandeep—with his greasy hair, his faded clothes and his revolting grin—standing in the distance. I wanted to turn around immediately but I knew that if I did so I would miss my bus. Besides, I didn't want to create a scene; what would Arun think? So I walked on, desperately hoping that maybe, with the strong Arun by my side, that jerk Mandeep wouldn't bother me.

'Fatso, if you eat any more of that ice cream you'll

burst,' Mandeep jeered.

I noticed Arun turning pink but he looked straight ahead, quickening his pace.

'Don't walk so fast, Munna, Munni won't be able to keep up. If she runs, there might be an earthquake.'

'Don't mind him,' said Arun. 'He's an asshole. It's best to just stay out of his way.'

As we hurried away, Mandeep followed us.

'Ahhh! Earthquake! Stop Godzilla before we all die!' he screamed and then laughed to himself.

Tears welled up in my eyes. Just my luck. Here I was, on my very first date, and Mandeep had to ruin it. I was surprised at Arun's reaction, but I could tell that he was uncomfortable and I wondered why a guy his size wasn't facing up to that rat.

I could not bear to finish my ice cream, not after what Mandeep had said, so I gave it to a stray dog. In my pain, I promised myself that one day, I would make Mandeep pay for all the grief and despair that he had caused me. I would have my revenge one way or another.

Prateek

The day started out as just another ordinary day: the usual difficulty waking up in the morning on a cold winter's day, and Ma screaming as I hopped out of bed just minutes before the bus arrived.

I sat through the first two classes, and even Jasmine Ma'am with her sweet silky voice, her hot body and her sleeveless blouses could not help me shake my lethargy away. By the third period, I was utterly fed up. I didn't really need to go to the toilet, but Sarita Ma'am's droning mathematical formulae were boring me to death and if I didn't go for a little jaunt, I would fall asleep at my desk. So I asked her permission to go to the toilet. I knew she wouldn't miss me, she was so absorbed in those formulae of hers that she didn't know who came and who went. I was loafing around the hall when I reached the girls' bathroom, and I saw that there was no one outside. The bathroom too seemed quiet, and I decided to take a peek inside—I had always wondered what it was like compared to the boys'. As soon as I entered, I heard some loud voices outside. I froze as they came closer and grew louder.

'Arre, look what we have here. Is this a little girl?' said Mandeep, the boy I feared most in school, though I had so far had the good luck of never meeting him.

'I, I was just leaving,' I said nervously, trying to sneak my way past him to the door.

'Not so fast, Munna. Where do you think you're going in such a hurry?' said one of Mandeep's sidekicks.

'I have to get back to class,' I said weakly, realizing that I sounded like a wuss.

'You aren't going anywhere, Munna, Not before we teach you a lesson for using the girls' bathroom without our permission,' Mandeep said with a cruel laughter.

He pulled out a short knife and held it close to my face.

'Take off your pants,' he said coldly.

Without a word, I quickly unfastened my belt, undid

my buttons, unzipped my pants and slid them down.

'Underwear too,' he said, an evil glint in his beady eyes.

With a great deal of discomfort, I slid my underpants down as well.

'And now for your lesson,' he said coldly, bringing the knife close to my penis.

I closed my eyes and prayed, tears welling my eyes, though I tried as hard as I could to prevent them from spilling over. And then I heard another voice.

'What do you think you guys are doing?'

I opened my eyes and breathed a sigh of relief. It was my friend Ranjit.

'Who the hell are you?' piped up one of Mandeep's two sidekicks.

'Looks like we'll have to teach this Munna a lesson as well,' said Mandeep with a grin.

Suddenly he pounced on Ranjit and held him against the wall, his hands around his throat. Ranjit coughed and I could hear him choking. I was so scared that I pissed in my pants.

'Munna has peed in his pants. He DESERVES to be in the girls' loo,' said one of the boys.

This distracted Mandeep who would have choked Ranjit to death. He let him go, looked at me and guffawed.

'Let's go, boys. Let these two clean up the mess,' he finally said.

And with that, Mandeep and his gang left, leaving Ranjit gasping for breath, and me standing with my pants in a pool of my own piss.

Ranjit

I heard myself scream in fear as they brought the knife close to my penis. I could feel the cold hard steel of that knife as they touched me to slice my organ into two.

I woke up drenched in a cold sweat, grateful that it was just a dream, but disgusted with myself because I was lying in a pool of my pee, and an image of Prateek came to my mind.

I cleaned myself and laid a towel on my bed. It was 3 a.m., but I couldn't go back to sleep, I could not forgive myself for what had happened to Prateek. He was one of my closest friends, and I hadn't been able to help him. Like a coward, I had backed off, getting beaten up instead of saving my friend. I didn't know what I should do or how I would do it, but I knew one thing—I had to take some steps one way or another. Should I try teaching the notorious Mandeep a lesson myself? Or should I tell the school authorities?

At breakfast the next morning I looked drained and tired; I hadn't slept all night.

'Are you okay, son?' asked my father, looking up from his newspaper and sipping his tea.

'Yes, Papa,' I said quietly, staring down into my cornflakes.

'You know, son,' he said, putting his newspaper aside, 'you can talk to me about anything. You shouldn't feel shy with your father.'

I was reluctant to discuss things with my father. I didn't

want him to think that his son was a wimp, but I was so unsure about what to do that I needed some direction.

'Papa, there is one thing...' I said, my voice shaking as I narrated the incident that had taken place in the girls' bathroom, between Prateek, Mandeep, his gang and me.

After a pause, my father smiled at me.

'Son, in my experience, bullies are the biggest cowards. You have to put them in their place, stand up to them. Once they know that you aren't scared of them, they won't bully again. This guy seems to be a real menace, and the dangerous sort too. I think that maybe you should tell the principal about it first and see what he does. If the school doesn't help then, let's revisit the problem.'

Though I was nervous and hesitant—after all I didn't want to get a reputation for being a sneak—I took my father's advice. I went to visit the principal, and complained about Mandeep.

Mandeep

I thought that I had been through hell with my father, but I was wrong. That evening, I got the worst beating that I had ever had in my life. A beating so bad that I ended up in the hospital with three ribs fractured.

Propped up on an uncomfortable bed in that grimy hospital full of shrieking, dying people, there was only one thing on my mind—revenge. I swore to teach two people the lesson of their lives—my father and that sneak Ranjit.

〜

I had realized that the best place to hide in when skipping classes was the administrative block because no one would expect to see a student there. I was walking past the principal's office and saw that little pipsqueak from the girls' bathroom waiting outside. The memory had me laughing out so loudly that a passing peon gave me an angry look. When I came by on my second round I passed him again, and that little runt had the audacity to look *me*, Mandeep Singh, in the eye, and even grin at me. I made a note of his behaviour and told myself that a visit to the girls' bathroom would have to be made very soon.

When I came home that evening, hoping to catch a few hours of TV before Papa came home, I saw his car outside. I hesitated to go inside but then, I thought that he would ask me too many questions if I came home late. I couldn't find him in his usual place—on the sofa next to the TV—so I went my room to change. I opened the door and saw him sitting on my bed, a scowl on his face.

He stood up when he saw me, took a belt of mine that was lying on the floor and without a word started to beat me. I considered running out of the room, but then wondered where I would run to, and if I did run, I would have to come back eventually and then I would get a bigger, worse beating than ever before.

As he beat me, he screamed at me. The school principal had called him and told them that I was a rogue, a menace who bullied kids. They were going to suspend me for a week, and if I was ever found bullying again, then I would be expelled. Usually he would stop when he saw blood, but today he kept on going, whipping me and thrashing me till I could take it no more, till I lay unconscious at his feet. The next thing I knew, I woke up at the hospital, my mother by my side.

I knew that Ranjit must have complained to the principal. I recalled that impish grin on his face and vowed to get out of here, and take revenge, however much that revenge cost me. I was back in school a few weeks later. I wasn't as strong as before, my ribs were still sore, but I was smart and quick, and I could fight the devil if I wanted to.

I followed his movements carefully, figuring out the best time and place to beat him up. I knew I had to be careful—I was injured, and I knew that these idiot teachers were watching me. I caught him on his way back from cricket practice. He was whistling, looking dandy, and tossing his cricket bat up into the air. I stood behind a wall, hockey stick in hand, waiting to get to him. I leaped at him when he got closer, and knocked the cricket bat out of his hands.

'Munna, you have guts, do you? You think a chutiya school principal can stop me? You have got to be crazy, Munna. NO ONE can stop Mandeep! I own this school!' I hit him as hard as I could, but the weight of the hockey stick and even the exertion of hitting him was too much for me. He lay there on the ground, clutching his face in his palms—a soft target for me. I would have done a far better job—after all this guy didn't fight back, didn't even say a word. But, I felt so tired that I thought I would faint.

Enough, I thought to myself; I could feel my blood in my mouth, so I spat on the sorry figure of Ranjit lying inert on the ground and I walked away.

Ranjit

Enough was enough! I was bruised but not badly hurt. When I thought he was just getting started, he stopped hitting me. I didn't know why, but I figured it was because he was afraid that if he beat me up too badly I would again complain about him.

But I didn't trust the system anymore. They hadn't done anything to protect me the first time or the second time, and I wouldn't give them a third chance. The only way now was to take things into my own hands.

I knew I couldn't do this alone. I wasn't a fighter, I had never been, but if I had a team, I knew that together we could teach that bully a lesson. I decided to ask Prateek and Arun, both of whom I knew had been bullied by Mandeep. I also knew that after the bathroom incident Prateek wanted revenge, almost as badly as I did. Arun was strong and athletic and we needed someone like him with us.

Arun agreed quickly and readily, a sweet smile dawning on his face when I told him about the plan. I hesitated when he suggested Roshni's name, but I thought about it carefully and finally agreed. Though it may slow us down, it would be good to have a girl on board. Moreover, Roshni was a topper; a fat, sweet, studious girl whom no one would suspect of bullying a miscreant like Mandeep. It might help save us from getting into trouble.

And so the four of us planned, plotted and schemed. Everyone had their own ideas about how we should tackle our tormentor. I listened carefully and reminded everyone of the final goal—we could punish him, thrash him, injure him, but ultimately we needed to make sure that he never ever bullied anyone. They all came up with good ideas, but they were too timid. Cricket bats, hockey sticks and leather belts wouldn't do the trick, we needed something else. And then the idea struck me.

I never saw my father use it, but I had often seen him hold it and polish it. He had had the revolver for as long as I could remember. He told me that it belonged to his father, an IPS officer, and that as a kid, he had always admired it. It reminded him of his father, of his strength, his courage and his dignity.

This was the gun that I would use to threaten that turd Mandeep. I imagined it with relish—I would hold the revolver to his head, and watch him beg for his life. He would never again dare bully any creature—human or animal.

At first they were taken aback, but I knew that I could convince the boys. I wasn't sure of Roshni, after all, girls and guns don't really go together, but strangely enough, she was the first to agree. She seemed thrilled by the idea of a gun being put to Mandeep's head. She said that she wanted to take her revenge her own way, something which involved chilli powder and eggs. Whatever made her happy, I figured.

On the other hand, Arun, whom we called 'the friendly giant', was the hardest to convince.

'What if...something happens?' he asked with concern.

'Nothing will happen, yaar. Trust me, this is the easiest and least violent way. Otherwise, we're going to have to hit him and there will be blood and shit. Who wants that mess?'

Prateek was quiet but I knew that he had my back.

We plotted in excruciating detail, thanks to Roshni who had tracked Mandeep's movements. At this point, we knew what he ate, what he drank and when he pissed. We planned everything, down to the second when we would approach him, threaten him and attack him.

Thinking of our revenge gave us all hope. As we edged closer to the chosen date, I could see them all become more confident. Roshni walked the corridors with confidence, Prateek got his mojo back, and Arun stopped slouching and walked with his head high.

D-day approached faster than we had imagined but we were all well, if not overly, prepared. Roshni had even made us do some online self-defence training. We were nervous, but exhilarated. I took my dad's gun from the box the previous night and wrapped it in a towel. I placed it carefully inside my backpack and locked that too. The school day passed slowly, too slowly, each minute dragging until, much to my relief, the closing bell rang. I sprinted to the football field where we had decided to meet.

The rest of them were as anxious as I was. We laughed nervously, high-fived each other and clutched our ammunition to our hearts. Prateek and Arun had hockey sticks, Roshni had her eggs and chilli powder, and I had my grandfather's gun.

We made our way to the park which Mandeep had to cross to get home. He lived close to school, twenty minutes away, and always walked alone. We had tracked his movements and we knew approximately when he would get to the park, but that day he was late and we waited anxiously.

'What if he doesn't come?' whispered Prateek in my ear. 'Our plan goes to the dogs?'

'Not really, yaar. We'll try again tomorrow,' I whispered back, though there was no need at all to whisper in the vast park which was empty, save for a few homeless people, probably drunk, who were resting in the shade of the trees.

Finally we saw him approach. As I stared at him intently, I saw that he had grown thin over the last few weeks. I hadn't noticed till now how weak and pale he looked. He was underweight and his shabby clothes hung on his skinny frame. He walked slowly with a limp, like an old man, as if each step was painful.

Mandeep made the job easier for us. He sat down on a park bench, taking his backpack off his shoulders, and putting his head into his hands. I looked at my three mates and gave them the signal. We ran towards him and surrounded him on all four sides.

'What the...' he looked up, his eyes wide with surprise.

Just for a second, he looked like a small, scared child, and for that instant I felt a pang of pity; but within seconds his face transformed and an evil grin stretched across his face.

'If it isn't the geek squad! You guys think you can take me on?' he said with a sneer. 'And fatso,' he said, looking at Roshni, 'you think you can do anything to me? You *can*. All you have to do is jump on me.'

He looked at Arun, stood up and pinched his cheek. 'You, Munna, you're an impotent prick. You think YOU can do anything to me?'

He laughed wildly and for a second I stood there in silence. And then he looked at me.

'Pipsqueaks are the worst. You watch what I do to you. Remember the girl's bathroom? Remember how you peed in your pants? Or wait, was that your friend? Do you need a diaper? I have one in my bag.'

I pulled out the gun from my pocket and pointed it at him.

'Achha, a gun. You think you can scare me with a *gun*? Stolen it from daddy, have you? Or is it a toy? If you pull the trigger, you might wet your pants like your friend!' he said with a high-pitched laugh, his eyes wild with anger, fear, or a combination of both.

I don't know what came over me, maybe it was his wild laughter, or the memory of Prateek and me in the girls' bathroom, drowning in our shame. I looked at Prateek, who was red with fear and embarrassment, and poor Roshni who was sweating like a pig; even Arun stood there with a confused expression on his face. A wave of anger swept over me, and I knew that there was one way, and only one way, to teach Mandeep a lesson, and I pressed the trigger. It was the easiest thing I had ever done in my life and just like that, without a sound, without a whimper, he fell to the ground.

Mandeep was killed on the spot. All four culprits were sent to a correctional facility for juvenile offenders. Their lives were ruined and their hopes for the future were dashed. Roshni could not go to the US on scholarship. Prateek, with a criminal record, could not apply to the IIT. Ranjit, who was awarded the longest sentence, could not apply to Delhi University. Arun who, all his life, had dreamed of serving his country by joining the Indian Army could never do so.

ಬ

Naaz

Naaz

The first thing that struck me was the smell—the sickly sweet smell of rotting vegetables mixed with the musky smell of sweating bodies. Every time I came back to India, I found the country changed—more buildings, more people, more cars, more lights, more chaos. But the smell, the smell always remained the same. I hated the visits to our hometown, Rohtak (Haryana). I hated our house—freezing in winter and hot in summer. I hated the pesky, inquisitive relatives and the long hours when I got tired of doing nothing at all. At least, I always knew that I would be going back home to New York, and that had kept me sane during those trips back home.

This time, though, the stench in Rohtak made me so nauseous that I almost fainted. I would have if Bhaiyya had not caught me in time and handed me a bottle of water. It wasn't only that the smell was worse than before.

Maybe, it was also that this time I knew it was going to be permanent. Papa had been transferred back to India, and this was now to be home. We had always known that, sooner or later, the move back was inevitable; after all, Papa was at New York University only for a teaching assignment. His stint had lasted five years, and in those five years, I had gone from being a child of ten to a young woman of fifteen. I didn't remember much of what I had left behind; my memories weren't very pleasant. I only remembered dusty roads, derelict houses, cars spewing exhaust fumes, annoying relatives with sharp tongues, and constant supplies of food. Though I loved to eat, I had maintained a strict diet, at least in New York where my aim was to be as skinny and lithe as possible since I was to try out for the cheerleading team. In Rohtak, there would be no cheerleading team, so, no pressure to maintain any sort of figure, and the only bright spot in all the darkness would be the food that was awaiting me.

Though there was nothing to look forward to, at least I had Aryan Bhaiyya, my best friend and closest confidant with me. AB, as I called him, seemed far less upset about moving to India than I was. In fact, he almost seemed to be looking forward to it. This was strange because, in the US, he was a popular kid; everyone loved the sporty, friendly, likeable guy. I thought he would be as distraught about leaving as I was, but then again, maybe he cared less because he was a guy, and guys always did care less about these things than girls did.

We moved back smack in the middle of the junior

college term which made matters even worse. I threw a fit about it, even refusing to go to college. I told my parents that I would work, earn my own money and then go back to my life in the US. My parents laughed at me and told me that in my head I was still living in America. In Rohtak, young girls didn't work; in fact, women in general did not work. They told me that if I wanted to go back, I had to work at it: I had to get good grades, build up my resumé, then I could apply to colleges in the US. In a way, this cheered me up, and though I had never been a good student, I vowed to work really hard so I could go back to the country that I loved.

Junior college in Rohtak was a world apart from my school in the US. For starters, we had to wear *school uniforms*—long dreary skirts that came down below the knees; loose white blouse; white socks which covered any remaining stretch of bare leg; gross black shoes and, worst of all, oil and plait our hair. The boys seemed to have a better deal: AB just wore a pair of pants, a collared shirt and sneakers. I had always loved fashion and clothes, and the thought of wearing this dreary uniform day in and day out made me utterly unhappy. I decided to give my uniform a facelift: I shortened my skirt by a few inches. I tailored my shirt to fit, and I even worked on the socks to make them a bit shorter. After my alterations, I felt much better about wearing the uniform.

Little did I know what a ruckus cutting a few inches off a hemline would create in Gargi Junior College, Rohtak. As I walked down the corridors, the girls made eyes at me, while the boys ogled. In the beginning, I didn't understand what was going on. Was this just the way it was here in India? Were people just this uncivilized, or was there something else going on? I decided to ignore the stares and go about my business. After all, what were these people to me?

A few days later, AB came to talk to me; an embarrassed look on his sweet face.

'Zee, I think you should re-tailor your skirt,' he said shyly, shuffling his feet and looking down at the floor.

'Why AB? Doesn't it look better this way? That bag which I wore earlier was just...I don't even know what to say about it.'

'These uniforms suck! But Zee, Rohtak is a strange place. People try to be really cool and stuff, but they are totally not. I think people are talking about you because of your skirt.'

'Rubbish, AB! How is that possible? You can hardly call my skirt short!'

'I'm telling you, Zee,' he said softly. 'I would never tell you otherwise. You know how I am about these things. Pretty chilled out.'

I saw him there with such a look of concern on his normally calm face that I agreed to re-tailor my uniform.

While the uniform incident seemed at that time like a silly, trivial one—after all it was just a hemline—it was revealing of the kind of close-minded, strange, parochial place that Rohtak was. If I had paid proper attention, I would have realized it, but I was stuck in a world of my own. Maybe it was denial, or maybe it was just lack of adjustment; whatever it was, even though I was physically in Rohtak, in my head I was still living in New York.

Junior College was not as awful as I had expected it to be. The girls were either shy or stuck up, and many of them even refused to talk to me. I came to know later that it was because they didn't understand my accent. Thankfully—as is typically always the case—the guys in Rohtak seemed cooler than the girls. AB, one class my senior in college, had made some interesting friends and they often came over to our place to play football in the backyard.

His friends were shy and sweet. They hardly spoke to me, were always polite when I spoke to them and just smiled at me from a distance. They stared a lot at me, but it seemed like everyone did that here in Rohtak; so I didn't think much about it, or let it disturb me.

Aryan

Naaz was so unhappy about moving back to Rohtak that I figured I should try to at least *appear* happy and put up a good front. It was incredibly hard to do so because I *hated* Rohtak and everything about it. Even though Naaz had created such a ruckus about moving back, now that we were here, she didn't seem to mind it. I noticed that, in some ways, she was enjoying the attention she was getting. I had heard a few boys whisper about her—she was hot stuff on the campus. After all, the arrival of a new girl from the US wearing short skirts was big news in Rohtak. I had never been the possessive kind of brother, and I figured it was harmless, and in a way maybe it was a good thing: she no longer seemed to be unhappy.

Unfortunately, unlike my sister, there was nothing in the slightest bit glamorous about me; so most of the kids at school tended to ignore me. It didn't help that they didn't understand a word of the American-accented English that I spoke, and they just laughed at my Hindi—a language in which I had lost proficiency during the past five years though I was trying very hard to get it back.

Life continued in a bland, monotonous way in Rohtak, and just when I was about to lose all hope and succumb to a lifetime of entertaining myself with computer and video games, I met Ronak.

I had often seen the clique of four hanging out in the hall of our college; they seemed to be a fun though rowdy lot—they played hooky, smoked cigarettes on the football field, and drank beer out of water bottles on the basketball court. They were well liked, these four, and though they often broke the rules, they didn't cause trouble, or get in anyone's way; at least it didn't seem so.

Football tryouts were in a week, and I desperately wanted to make it to the football team. It would give me a way to interact with some people. But it wasn't going to be as easy as I had thought. The boys in Rohtak were surprisingly good and I had seen them practice. Also, I was totally out of shape—all the dal makhani and butter chicken cooked in cow's butter (our own cow to be precise) were doing nothing for me. Since I had no friends and Naaz was really no good at football, though she did try, I could only practice by myself.

It was during one evening of solo practice that I saw Ronak and his mates smoking weed on the football field. They were far away from me, and I tried my best to avoid them and instead focused on getting the ball into the goal. But I was rusty; the football had a mind of its own and it rolled over to them.

When I went over to retrieve my football, I was met with a friendly smile, totally unexpected.

'Dude, want some?' Ronak asked, offering me a joint.

'Uh...' I said, holding my football, deciding what to do.

'Come on, dude, no formality,' said the guy sitting beside him.

'Sure, thanks,' I said, taking the joint from them. I didn't do weed very often; I had never really liked it, but I knew that this would be a good way to break the ice.

I took a long drag, suppressing a cough. I didn't want them to think I was an amateur and then, when I was about to walk away, Ronak called out to me.

'What's your name, bro?'

'Aryan,' I said, reaching out to shake each guy's hand as they introduced themselves.

'We're going to watch some cool stuff at Nab's,' said Ronak. 'Wanna join?'

'Uh, sure,' I said. They seemed like nice fellows, and here was finally a chance to make some friends.

It turned out that Nab lived in the same complex as I did, and as we walked over, we chatted a little bit. They were friendly, and I saw they were all trying hard, speaking in their strained and accented English. I *did* speak Hindi of sorts and I thought it would be easier for them so I tried to switch over, but they seemed keen on speaking to me in English. It was a strange sort of ego thinking. They asked me from where I had moved here and whether I liked it. They had seen Naaz and me in school, and when I told them that we were both a little lonely, they were all kinder than I had expected. They put their arms around me and reassured me that I now had friends, brothers, so there was no need to worry.

At Nab's house, we all huddled around an old laptop in his tiny, cramped room filled with stuff. It looked like we were here to watch porn downloaded off the internet. Boys will be boys, I thought to myself with a smile, no matter where in the world. From NYC to Rohtak, it seemed all guys had one thing on their minds. After thirty minutes of watching fuzzy, poor-quality porn, I offered my own collection—the latest American porn downloaded off high-speed internet.

Within minutes, all four boys were at my place. My parents were out visiting my grandparents while Naaz was sitting in the drawing room watching TV. She was wearing the shorts and tank top she wore around the house—an outfit to which I had never given a second thought. But when I introduced my four new mates to her, I could feel a palpable tension in the air. I knew immediately that they weren't used to seeing girls in shorts, but I didn't think much of it then. After all, they were bashful with Naaz, not even meeting her eye, but looking down at the floor and blushing when I introduced them. After that, we all went up to my room to begin a friendship that I hoped would lift me out of my misery.

Ronak

We had unanimously decided that Naaz was the hottest girl in Rohtak and that, come what may, we had to nail her. It wasn't only for our enjoyment, but for hers too. After all, girls like her probably enjoy it and need it. And so my buddies and I decided that this term we would embark on 'Mission Naaz'.

The key to Naaz was obviously her brother Aryan. We could see by the way the poor guy loafed around alone that he had no friends. So we decided to rope him in. One day, we followed him to the football field and offered him some weed. From then on, there was no turning back. He took to our group immediately (who wouldn't?) and even invited us to his home. With his home came the desirable Naaz, who was equally lonely.

The minute I laid my eyes on her in the shorts and tank top she was wearing* and with her big breasts), I knew that I had to have her. I hadn't seen anything like her before. I didn't know much about her then, but as I observed her over the coming days, I knew that my initial opinion had been spot on—she was a loose-moralled American girl; the kind we saw in the movies, the kind who liked to have some fun.

Naaz

They looked like nice guys. After all, AB had always had nice friends with whom I had invariably gotten along and often made my own. I had been finding it so difficult to make friends that I was thrilled when he brought the boys over. Like all the boys whom I had encountered here, they were supremely shy; but they seemed friendly, and I even found Ronak hot, in a rugged sort of way.

They came over often, especially since my house was largely parent-free. Dad was in the office till late every day, and Mom, she was having a gala time in Rohtak visiting all her relatives. We became friends, AB, his pals and I. My conversations with them tended to be a little stilted because their English wasn't very good; but they *always* made it a point to speak with me in English, and I sort of enjoyed their company. I figured some friends were better than none at all.

When they weren't huddled in AB's room (I often wondered what they did there because I was never invited in his room), we played games—either football or cards. We led a peaceful coexistence till one day Mom returned unexpectedly early from my maasi's place.

The boys had needed an even number of players to play a match, and even though I wasn't in the mood to play football, all five of them, including AB and Ronak (on whom I had a minor crush, mostly because of lack of other options) begged me, so I joined in. I was wearing what I usually wore in Rohtak's heat—a tank top and shorts. It had been an unusually fun match, and though I wasn't as good as the rest of them, I had played actively, even scoring a goal. I was so happy after scoring my goal, that I hugged my teammates, Ronak and Nab. They seemed a little surprised, I do admit, but in the heat of the moment everything passed quickly.

Mom saw this from the verandah, and when I came back inside, I had to face her anger.

'Naaz, come here,' she said sternly. Hearing the tone of her voice, I knew that something was wrong.

'Yes, Mom?'

'Why were you hugging that boy like that? WHY were you even playing football with them? And what are you *wearing*?' she asked me coldly.

'Mom! What's wrong with playing football? I played *every* day in New York. I don't go around hugging boys randomly! I SCORED A GOAL. That's what you do when you score a goal. And I'm wearing what I wear *every* single day.'

'Naaz, I thought you had more sense than that. You do all this in New York, *not* in Rohtak! This is a very different kind of place, you can't do all this hug-shug here,' she said, now screaming at me.

'I can't believe you, Mom. FIRST, you move me to this God-forsaken place, and now that I've FINALLY made friends, you are shouting at me. What the *hell* am I supposed to do?'

I ran up to my room, hot tears streaming down my cheeks. All the stuff that I had been holding in—the anger, the loneliness, adjusting to an alien culture—all of it came to the surface and I cried my eyes out. Far more than fighting with Mom, I think I needed a good cry.

Over the next few days, things got better. I think my whole family felt bad for me and then, like a godsend, Mom and Dad announced that they were going to a wedding, which I couldn't attend because it fell smack in the middle of my exams. I was glad because, I needed some time alone, away from my family. For once I was happy that even AB would be going.

They left the following week, leaving me a million instructions. I was happy to see the car finally pull away, and I settled in front of the TV with my books, for a *Sex and the City*-cum-studying marathon.

All was good, but for only about one day, and then I started feeling lonely and bored. At one point I even thought of going over to my grandmother's place, but the thought of twenty relatives pinching my cheeks and commenting on my clothes made me quickly change my mind; so I decided to stay at home and study.

It was early in the evening, only 5 p.m., and I had already finished my studies for the next day's exam. I decided to take a little walk in my colony and get some fresh air. Just minutes outside my house, I ran into Ronak and the gang. I was glad to see them; they weren't the most engaging company, but at this point *anyone* would do.

'What are you guys up to?' I asked.

It was Ronak who had the best English, and who always replied on behalf of the group.

'Nothing, just roaming around, thinking what to do. What about you?'

'Getting bored. Bhaiyya and parents are out of town, so just taking a walk.'

'Oh, okay,' said Ronak, shuffling his feet in the dirt.

'You guys want to come over?' I asked hopefully. 'We could watch a movie or play some game.'

Ronak looked at his mates and then he nodded his head vigorously, his face gleaming with gleeful delight. And we made our way over to my house.

Ronak

Everyone knows that there is only one reason why a girl like Naaz would invite four boys over to her house, and that is to have sex. We could see she wanted it—her clothes, the way she sat on the sofa, these small signs said it all.

She chose some funny English movie that none of us understood but through which we sat, waiting for an opportunity to strike.

We went out to the garden to smoke while Naaz went to the toilet.

'"Mission Naaz", tonight,' I declared with confidence to my mates.

Arjun and Rakshay looked a little concerned but my main man Nab was in. The two of us were a tag team, and I knew we could convince them.

'Don't be chutiyas, yaar. She wants it, can't you see it in her eyes?'

'I don't know, yaar,' said Arjun. 'We could get into a lot of trouble.'

'What are you saying, bro? Girls like her, they are like Draupadi, and we...we're like her husbands. Four, but with the strength of five,' I said with a wink.

'You guys decide what you want, but Ronak and I are doing it,' said Nab with finality. He put out his cigarette and we walked back into the house, with the confidence of a hundred tigers.

She sat there in her skimpy skirt, her legs long and sexy, as she waited for us to come and get her. We knew she might create a ruckus, after all, girls always did; but we would just have to shut her up.

Nab and I sat down next to her on the small sofa. She looked surprised, but she didn't move, not at first. Slowly and steadily, we moved closer to her and I placed my hand on her knee. She looked surprised but didn't say anything and before I could do more she got up and left.

I wasn't going to let this one go so easily, so I followed her into the kitchen where she was pouring herself a glass of water. I went up to her, grabbed her head and brought it close to mine, kissing her on the mouth. She pushed me away.

'Get away from me! What *are* you doing, Ronak?'

'I'm only doing what you want me to do, baby,' I said, wanting her even more badly now than before. Anger suited her.

She was walking away from me back into the drawing room, and I knew that there was only one way to handle this. I followed her and picked her up from behind, putting my hand over her mouth and hoisting her over my shoulder even as she kicked and scratched me.

'Chalo, boys,' I said, calling my mates. Nab was quick to follow and he took hold of her legs as I held her mouth and arms. Arjun and Rakshay looked scared but they followed.

'Can't you see she wants it?' I said to them with a wink.

We tied a towel over her mouth to drown out the noise, and Nab held her legs as I tore off her clothes. Her body was as deadly as I had imagined it would be. I stroked it all over, before unzipping my jeans, taking them off and then, with all my might and strength, diving inside her. Once I was finished, Nab took over, and then we persuaded Arjun and Rakshay to take turns. By the time they did her, she was quiet, not trying to throw them off or kick them off; so they had an easier time than we did.

'"Mission Naaz" accomplished,' I said, high-fiving my boys. By the time we left she was asleep or something; she just lay on the sofa, making an occasional whimpering sound or two.

Aryan

I could sense something was wrong the second I stepped into the house. There was a strange stillness, an unnerving quiet, a weird chill in the air. Naaz was in her bedroom, sleeping, though it was two o'clock in the afternoon. She had never been one to sleep during the day, and so Mom was immediately worried about her. It turned out that Naaz was sick—she had a fever though there was no apparent reason for infection, and she was pale and weak. There were also bruises on her arms. Mom took her to see a doctor; but he said it was only viral, and prescribed some pills. He also said it was to be expected, her body was adjusting to the environment. Given the nature of her temporary unwellness, I didn't think too much about her not talking to me or not coming to have meals with us. What bothered me more was that my new friends refused to talk to me. They were cold and aloof, and I wondered whether I had done something wrong. I reached out to them a few times but they would have nothing to do with me; in fact, even when they saw me in school, they ignored me. I was worrying so much about this that I didn't pay any notice to Naaz.

Only after a week did I notice that something was very wrong with my sister. She had lost a lot of weight; she was pale as a ghost and she hardly spoke to anyone. She would not look me in the eye. When I asked her whether she was okay, she just mumbled back to me. She told Mom that she was too unwell to go to junior college, and she moped around the house all day. When Mom told her that she had no fever or illness and that she had to go back to school, Naaz had a violent outburst and then a breakdown. I had never seen her behave this way before, not even when we were leaving America.

I decided that I really needed to figure out what was up with her, and so I mustered up courage, went to her room and knocked on her door. When she opened it, I could tell that she had been crying. Her eyes were teary and swollen, her nose was red and running; all in all, she looked pretty awful.

Without my even saying anything she hugged me, and started crying. I froze. I knew then that something really terrible had happened to my sister.

Naaz

For days I was numb, unfeeling. I felt as if I were stuck in a nightmare that I hoped would end very soon. But it was unending and the more I moped, the more I kept to myself, the deeper I sank into depression. I didn't want to tell anyone or talk to anyone. I only wanted to be by myself, alone, because a part of me kept on saying that this nightmare would soon end. But it didn't, it just got darker and darker, till one day, even though I had said that I would not, I told AB everything. Once I did, I felt as if a huge weight had been lifted off my shoulders, but I also felt more scared. What would happen now? AB was shocked, angry, violent, sad. He broke down and, holding his head in his hands, he blamed himself for everything: for befriending those criminals, for bringing them home, for his poor judgement. But unlike me, despite being devastated, he took action, beginning by telling my parents. Papa did not want to go to the police, he did not trust them at all. He thought that we should deal with it ourselves, instead of turning it into a public scandal handled by inept authorities. Mom, on the other hand, who was both livid and crying at the same time, put her foot down and told him that she would move heaven and earth to make sure that those boys got sentenced, and for that to happen we had to seek redress and justice.

And justice we did get. Within weeks, all four boys were charged with rape. Nab, Arjun and Rakshay were sentenced to lifetime terms in prison. Ronak, who was below eighteen, was sent to a juvenile correctional centre. The judge, a kind old lady, assured us that she would ensure that he got his due punishment though it looked unlikely at the present moment. In one way, I was satisfied with the outcome of the trial, but in another, I knew that it didn't really matter because something fundamental within me had been destroyed, and no one—no lawyer, no judge, no arm of justice—could restore that.

∽

Together We Live, Together We Die

What *was* it about her that had got him so bad? Prima facie, she was ordinary—medium height, shoulder-length hair, fair skin, cute, button-like features; but nothing particularly eye-catching. She looked a few years younger than her sixteen years, probably because she was so thin: her waist was so small that he could put both his hands around it and have the tips of his fingers touch each other. Despite her utter normality, every time he saw her, his heart beat like a rap song, irregularly and with loud thuds that sometimes made him break into a sweat.

It hadn't always been like that. In the beginning, Ankit and Mehak were ordinary friends, if you could even call them that. They were clubbed to work on a project, and they both grumbled. Ankit didn't want to work with a girl, and Mehak, a star student, didn't want to work with a fresher who would potentially bog down her and her report. But as they worked together they realized that they made a great team. While Ankit was great at conception, ideation and outlines, Mehak was fabulous at putting it all together with artwork and graphics; and they created a geography project which won them the top prize.

Love didn't happen to them gradually; it sneaked up on them suddenly, with a bang, taking them both totally by surprise. On a boring, ordinary day, as Ankit sat in the library idling away his time, he saw Mehak sitting quietly in a corner, her nose stuck in a Harry Potter book. And as he looked at her, *stared* at her really, he felt a shiver run down his spine, a tingling in his fingers and a strange throbbing in his groin. He didn't understand what was happening to him, but he couldn't take his eyes off her, and the more he looked at her the more he realized how beautiful she was. Over the next few days, Mehak noticed the change: from that cock-sure, bored guy he had been when she first met him, he was now attentive and shy around her. She felt something stir in her towards this new Ankit and, without even realizing it, she started having feelings for him.

And as their friendship blossomed into romance, they became awkward around each other. She became aware of how untidy her hair was and how oily her skin was. Ankit became conscious of the fact that he had body odour (what must the sweet-scented Mehak think of that!) and that his pants were two sizes too big. Just like that, the jovial camaraderie and light-hearted banter that they had always exchanged went out of the window. Ankit started noticing things that he had never noticed about Mehak: her well-shaped eyebrows, her sparse eye-lashes (but so attractive nonetheless), the way her lips curved into a perfect smile, and the way she puckered her mouth and bit her lip when she was trying to focus. She realized how cute Ankit was. His glasses, which she had once thought of as dorky, suddenly seemed cute; his persona, which she once thought was unimpressive, suddenly seemed charming; and the body odour which had repelled her was replaced with a saffron cologne of which she started dreaming. And so, in the days following their prize-winning project, Ankit and Mehak graduated from friends to boyfriend and girlfriend.

They were in the throes of young love, and both of them seemed to be living in a world made for two. They woke up to thoughts of each other, they day-dreamt their way through class trying to steal glances at each other without making it too obvious, and had hasty conversations during the break. They waited for the school closing bell to ring so that they could meet and ride the bus home together. When they got home, they SMSed and chatted online till they fell asleep thinking of each other.

It was easy for Ankit. His parents, having married for love, were far more liberal than most parents. They were happy that Ankit seemed to have settled into his new school in such a short while. It was harder for Mehak; her parents were conservative and since she was an only child, she bore the full brunt of their attention. There was hardly a moment when her parents' energies weren't focused on her. All Mehak Rathore's parents wanted was that their brilliant daughter should be number one in her studies and become a doctor. She was intelligent and hardworking, so it wasn't difficult for her to do well, and there wasn't a single year when she had not been at the top of her class. Until now, her parents' goals had been her goals too; but then she had met Ankit, and he had changed her world, her perspective, her dreams. She realized that young people like her *could* have their own lives, their own dreams. She was inspired by Ankit, who wanted to become a wildlife photographer. Until now, she had lived only for her parents, but now with Ankit in her life she felt that the direction of her life had changed.

Before they knew it, five months had passed by and they had reached the end of the semester; it was gruelling exam time. But before the exams, there was one thing to which every student looked forward, and that was the annual class trip—an overnight journey to Sindhudurg fort. Ankit was thrilled at the prospect because it meant that he could spend an uninterrupted twenty-four hours with Mehak but, much to his disappointment, her parents were proving to be an obstacle.

'Is there NO way you can convince your father?' complained Ankit to a distraught Mehak.

'My parents, yaar...they have *never* allowed me go on a trip like this. I've been trying for five long years but no luck yet. They tell me that I should focus on my studies.'

'Why do they have to be like this, it's the *last* time, yaar. In senior school we won't have these anymore,' whined Ankit.

'Ankit, please don't make me feel *worse* than I am already feeling. You know I'm dying to go on this trip,' said Mehak, a little annoyed. It seemed to her that Ankit was blaming her partly for not being able to go, when the truth was, there was nothing she wanted more badly right now than that.

'You're right, Baba,' said Ankit softly. 'It's not your fault. It's just that the idea of spending time with you is... amazing. Think about it, we could sneak out in the evening, go for walks on the beach, explore the fort together...just thinking about it makes me so happy.'

'Just thinking about *not* going makes me feel awful,' said Mehak. 'So, please let's not.'

'Okay, fine. But promise me you'll at least try to persuade your father. Don't give this up without a fight.'

'I promise,' conceded Mehak though she was all but sure that her father would refuse.

Fuelled by her conversation with Ankit, Mehak decided to speak with her father at dinner.

'Papa, have you been to Sindhudurg fort?' asked Mehak as she ladled tomato soup into her bowl.

'Hmph!' grunted her father, which was his way of saying yes.

'How was it?' she asked.

'Like any other fort,' he said, more focused on the contents of the paper that he was reading than on speaking with her.

'I guess I wouldn't know, I've never been to any fort,' said Mehak quietly. She added, 'I would love to go.'

'If you get good marks, then, Mummy and I will take you there,' said Mr Rathore, distracted by an interesting piece of news.

'Papa, actually...my school is going there this weekend.'

'Good for them. These school trips are for rowdy children; good children don't go on such trips.'

'Papa, that's not true at all. I'm the only one in my class who is not going. I'm not the only good child in my class, you know.'

'See? That is the difference between you and them. There is a reason why *you*, not they, are the topper,' said Mr Rathore with pride.

'Papa, I'm the only one in my class who doesn't ever do *anything*, I never go on any trips, attend any parties; I hardly have any friends. And that too although I have been doing so well in my studies lately.' Thinking about it made Mehak so unhappy that, unable to control herself, she burst into tears and, leaving the dinner table, ran up to her room.

Feeling sorry for herself, she was crying her eyes out when her father came and knocked on her door.

'Come in,' she said through her tears.

'Beta,' said her father gently. 'I did not know you wanted to go so badly. Of course if you want to go you can go. I give you permission. Just promise to be careful, and take your books. I don't want your grades slipping because of this.'

'Are you serious, Papa?' said Mehak, a smile breaking out on her tear-stained face. She had never expected this sort of a reaction from her usually strict father. The tears, it seemed, had done their job.

She wiped her tears and as soon as her father left her room, Mehak called Ankit.

'Good news, Anku! We are going to Sindhudurg!'

'Are you serious?' said Ankit in disbelief. He hadn't expected this at all, especially after what Mehak had told him about her father.

'Yes! I convinced Papa,' said Mehak gleefully.

'You're the best! See, I told you, you can charm anyone...'

Sindhudurg I convinced Papa.ndhudurg, so, I am changing it here and hereafter. was everything that Ankit and Mehak had expected, and more. There was only one young, junior teacher on the trip, who seemed to be on her phone the entire time, and hardly cared what the students did. Everyone in their class knew about their relationship by now, so most of them left them alone. Mehak and Ankit abandoned the group more than once and went to do their own thing. They explored the lovely old fort of Sindhudurg, took long walks on the beach and visited the only coconut tree in the world whose branches bore fruit.

The two lovers packed a small lunch and had it under a verdant, grassy hill. They spent a few hours together, hugging each other, looking into each other's eyes, happy and content in each other's company.

'I love you, Mehak,' said Ankit softly and then, suddenly, he stood up and grabbed her hand. 'Come with me,' he said, 'I have an idea.'

'Arre! What's come over you?' exclaimed Mehak, giggling as she ran to keep up with him.

Ankit kept walking fast till he reached a small deserted temple. No one had been here in a while; all the idols were broken, and there was a lot of trash lying around. There was an eeriness about the whole place which Mehak didn't particularly like.

'Let's get out of here, Ankit. This place is freaking me out!'

'Not before you marry me,' he said with a smile.

'Marry you!' exclaimed Mehak.

'Yes. Mehak Rathore, will you marry me?' asked Ankit, going down on one knee, a smile on his face.

Before she could say anything, he slipped a small ring made of grass around her finger.

'Anku, you're so silly!' said Mehak with a laugh though she was struck by how romantic he was. That's what she loved about him; he never failed to surprise her.

'Do I have the option of saying no?' she asked.

'Not really,' he replied. He got up and gave her a light kiss on the cheek.

He led her by the hand around a broken Shiv Ling and laughingly they performed the seven pheras around it to solemnize their pretend marriage.

'From this day on you're my wife, and I'm your husband,' said Ankit before enveloping Mehak in a bear hug. 'No one can keep us apart, not even Mr Rathore,' said Ankit with a grin.

'I love you, Anku,' said Mehak gently, stepping into his arms, happier than she had ever been in her life.

For the next few weeks, they were both busy preparing for the exams. Both Ankit and Mehak were serious students and wanted to score well. With each other's support, they studied even harder than before. The only drawback was that they hardly saw each other since they were on study leave and weren't going to school, and it was difficult for Mehak to go out. They both knew that after their exams they would have a long and free summer, and this thought kept them motivated to study hard.

The day after their first English exam, Ankit walked Mehak to her bus stop, happy to have a few minutes with her before the bus came. He would see her again only after five days, and that seemed much too far away.

That same afternoon, Mehak's father decided to pick his daughter up from the bus stop. He had a half-day off, and Mehak, poor thing, had been studying so hard. This way, he could spend a little time with her and maybe quiz her on some chemistry, his favourite subject. He arrived early and was waiting for the crowd of students to approach so he could spot Mehak, when he saw a boy and a girl standing together in the distance, holding hands. He looked disapprovingly at the brazen couple, and then, as he drove closer to the bus stop, he saw the girl come close to the boy and kiss him on the lips. He was disgusted and decided to write a letter to the school authorities complaining about this lewd behaviour, when his look froze on the face of the young smiling girl. For a second he couldn't believe his eyes. Could it be? It was unthinkable that this shameless girl who could kiss a boy, and that too in a public place in broad daylight, should be his very own daughter.

He pushed down on the brakes, and then suddenly after a moment zoomed forward, bringing the car to a sudden halt, leaving a stream of cars honking angrily behind him. He then walked up to Mehak and without a word dragged her into the car.

She didn't leave her room for three days and three nights, and didn't put a morsel of food into her mouth; all she did was lie in bed staring at the ceiling. She also did something which she had never ever done in her life—she missed her mathematics exam. She would have continued her fast until death, protesting her father's behaviour, but her survival instincts were stronger than her sadness. She knew that if she missed one more exam she would be held back, and she would have to repeat Class XI. This would keep her away from her beloved Ankit, and she couldn't possibly bear that. So finally, Mehak managed to get out of bed, brush her teeth, put on some clean clothes, eat some food and sit down to study. For the first time in a week, she switched on her cell phone and went online. She was bombarded with messages from an anxious and angry Ankit. She feared that her mother might be eavesdropping, so she sent Ankit a text message asking him to come online to chat. The virtual world, it seemed, was the only safe place for her and Ankit now.

Over chat she told him everything, about what had happened after her father dragged her away, how he had beaten her up so badly that she had bled. On video chat she showed him the ugly, purple bruises that were all over her arms and stomach. Worse than the beatings, she said, were the names he had called her. She didn't want to repeat them; it was too painful for her. She told him how awful things had been since then—she hadn't eaten, hadn't really slept, but had lain in bed, thinking of him.

Mehak hadn't thought about how Ankit would react to her father's behaviour, but she hadn't expected him to be *this* angry and she had certainly not thought he would come, at that very instant, to her house for a face-off with her father. When he disappeared online, she attributed it to a faulty internet connection; but twenty minutes later, she heard the doorbell ring.

Her father opened the door to a fuming Ankit; and when she heard his voice, she ran downstairs.

'How dare you, Mr Rathore?' screamed Ankit. 'Do you know it is illegal to beat children like this? You could be arrested for it!'

'Who the hell do you think you are?' said her father, quivering with anger. 'You were molesting my daughter. I could have YOU thrown in jail, you bastard!' he shouted.

'Your daughter and I are in love! You may not accept it, but it's the truth. Nothing can keep us apart, not even you!' said Ankit, so angry that he could hardly speak. He was on the verge of tears.

Without another word, Mr Rathore banged the door shut and walked away.

He had not seen her, and at this point she felt as if she may just faint, so she slipped back to her room to call Ankit.

That night, when she went down to get a glass of water, she heard her father talking to her mother in their bedroom. She heard him mention her name, so she sneaked closer to the door. She was astonished to hear her father sobbing quietly and telling her mother how bad he felt for beating up their daughter.

'God has given me such a good, pure daughter. How could have I done this? It's as if a demon got into me when I saw her with that boy.'

After a brief silence her father continued.

'What she did was wrong, but these days children are easily influenced. I don't blame her completely, but she needs to focus on her studies. She can't waste her time on boys and other frivolous things. Not right now at least.'

'She's a good student, and has always been,' said her mother softly.

'I know, but I am going to send her to the US for her studies. There are no two ways about it, and to get into a good American college, you have to be a topper. Our Mehak can't be distracted, not now. We MUST keep her away from that boy. He's not a good boy at all; he will keep her from pursuing her studies and will end up ruining her life. The only way to fix things is to send her to America.'

'But that is so far away,' whispered her mother.

'Yes, the farther she gets away from that boy, the better,' said her father with more confidence now.

'America?' thought Mehak, going back to her room.

America...that would be thousands and thousands of miles away from her love. Ankit's parents could certainly not afford to send him to the US, and she knew how her father was—once he set his mind on something, it was close to impossible to change it. The more she thought

about it, the more depressed she became. She would rather
die than be so far away from the boy she loved more than
her life. She could not possibly go away.

She sent Ankit an SMS, asking him to come online.

Mehak: They want to send me to America, Anku.

Ankit: What! You serious? Since when?

Mehak: Since the whole bus thing, I guess. I
don't know. But they want to keep me as far away
from you as possible.

Ankit: What's their problem, yaar? My parents
are cool about it; why can't yours be?

Mehak: My parents are different, Anku…you KNOW
how they are. But I can't do anything about it.
It sucks.

Ankit: My darling wife…how can I live without
you, if you go away from me?

Mehak: I won't be able to live without you,
either. It's not possible. Together we live,
together we die, Ankit. Remember the promise we
made to each other the day we got married at
Sindhudurg?

Ankit: A promise is a promise.

He pulled out the grass ring that he kept in his pocket
at all times and showed it to Mehak on video chat.

With great difficulty Mehak got out of bed to appear
for her exam the next morning. Though there was nothing
wrong with her physically, she felt so sick and weak that
she could hardly walk; the thought of leaving Ankit was
simply devastating. They had planned to meet after their

exam, and when she saw Ankit, she knew that he felt the same way. He was unshaven, paler than she had ever seen him before, and there were dark circles under his eyes.

She didn't care who was watching and she stepped into his arms to give him a hug.

'I can't live without you,' she whispered as tears ran down her face.

'I can't either,' said Ankit hoarsely, on the verge of tears himself.

They thought of it as an act of ultimate commitment—after all, it was what they had promised each other at the temple. Together, they would prove to the world and all the people who obstructed their love, how much they loved each other. They were kindred souls who had been together in past lives, and would be together in the next. If it wasn't working out in this lifetime, it would work out in the next. It was in this spirit of love that they made a pact and solemnized it—together we live, together we die, they swore to each other.

They wanted to be together even in their final moments; so they switched on their video cameras, which had been the vehicle of their love. It was a drastic step, but it was the only way to seal their love and make it eternal. It was the only way to show Mehak's parents the purity of their love.

They each took a dupatta and tied one end around their necks, the other end firmly tied to the ceiling fan. They stood steady on their respective chairs, looking at each other intently on their computer screens and said a final 'I love you'.

Mehak lifted one leg and stood poised to take the other off. Ankit, with his eyes shut, stepped off the chair and kicked it away. She froze, and stood in that state for a few seconds, staring in disbelief at the video camera and at the image of Ankit's body dangling from the fan, like a fragile leaf.

And before she knew it, she had torn the dupatta off her neck, stepped off the chair and jumped onto the floor. She ran out of her room to find her father, her face a mask of frozen fear. It was too late by the time Ankit's father broke open the door to the locked room. His son was already dead.

Mehak slipped into a deep depression, and had to be admitted to a mental institution. She kept a picture of him by her bedside; she kept the notes and cards that he gave her under her pillow. She was dying a slow death; every time she thought of him—which was almost all the time—she felt a dagger stab her through the heart. She couldn't get her head around what had happened: Ankit, her best friend, her soulmate and the boy with whom she had meant to spend the rest of her life was dead, and she was the one who had killed him.

ॐ

Honour

The wedding festivities were in full swing; the shehnais were being played, the guests were mingling, the food was being devoured, and the grandeur of the wedding was being admired by all. In short, things were going smoothly, or as smoothly as one could expect at a wedding. Most importantly, at least to me, was that Namrata Di seemed to be on top of the world, and though she had met Tushar Bhaiyya only once, they both seemed to be very much in love. Her marriage had been arranged, the way she had expected and wanted her entire life. My parents had thought that he would make a good match for their daughter: he was from the right caste, his family owned a large farm and they lived just nine kilometres away from us in a house which was larger than ours. Papa had always told us that a girl should settle into a bigger family, a family with 'a higher status than her own', and Tushar Bhaiyya's family fit the bill. It was the first wedding in our family so Papa had pulled out all the stops, more than he should have and when Ma reprimanded him about the expenditure, he was indignant.

'She is our eldest daughter and our reputation is at stake. Moreover, after they see how we throw a wedding, matches for Shobha will be lined up outside our door,' he said gleefully. I cringed when I heard him.

While Namrata Di's ambition in life had been to get married, I detested weddings, and I wondered how I would ever go through my own. Though my parents had tried to persuade me otherwise, my goal in life was never marriage. I wanted to work, be successful, make money on my own and be respected. Some would have thought me selfish, but I didn't want my life to be only about marriage, husband, kids. I wanted it to be about myself.

'Shobha, where have you been?' asked Charu, Tushar Bhaiyya's sister, jolting me out of my thoughts. 'Everyone is looking for you! The pheras are starting.'

I looked at my phone. Damn, it was almost the muhurat time.

'You're right, Charu. I'm so sorry. Is Ma angry?' I asked worried, imagining my mother's irritation at my disappearance.

'No Di, nothing like that. It's just that they were wondering where you were. No one has seen you for the last hour,' she said with a laugh.

It was true; I had needed some time off from the chaos and had been wandering about alone, musing rather than receiving guests as Ma had asked me to do.

'Come on now, otherwise we'll be late,' she said taking my hand and directing me towards the mandap.

I liked Charu, more than I liked Tushar Bhaiyya. Namrata Di had been besotted by him in an instant. He was after all the 'gora, chitta' boy she had always imagined for herself. It was harder to win my heart though. I thought there was something odd about him, I couldn't place my finger on it. He was polite and sweet enough to me, but there was something in that brooding look of his which I didn't quite understand.

'Beta, where were you? Namrata has been looking everywhere for you,' said my mother.

Now I felt guilty. This was the most important day in my sister's life, and the least that I could do was to be there for her. I went up to Di, removed some loose flower petals from her blouse, and squeezed her hennaed hands, swearing to myself that come what may, I would always be by her side.

The pheras lasted much longer than I expected, only ending at 1 a.m. By this time I was *starving*. I hadn't eaten a morsel of food since morning, and the food here looked good. While the two families were congratulating each other, hugging and thumping each other's back, I sneaked away to get a quick bite before I quite literally fainted of starvation.

The numerous varieties of food had me confused— Indian, Chinese, Continental and even Thai. As I walked around the buffet tables, filling my plate as quickly as I could, I bumped into a young man, and the bowl of dal on my plate spilled all over his shirt.

'I'm so sorry,' I said, aghast at my clumsiness, staring

at the yellow liquid dripping from his white shirt to his black pants.

I put my plate down on the floor, trying to wipe the dal off his shirt with my napkin.

He laughed. 'No problem. We have a few extra uniforms here,' he said.

Uniforms, I wondered, and then noticed that he was wearing a waiter's uniform; though in no way did he look or sound like a waiter.

I stood confused, the soiled napkin in my hand.

'Hi, I'm Harshad,' he said, extending his hand to me. For the first time I looked up at him, and his handsome face had me staring for a few seconds—grey-green eyes, a Roman nose, lovely straight teeth, bronzed skin—this guy was one of the nicest-looking men I had seen in my life.

'I, uh, I'm Shobha,' I said, bringing my limp hand to his.

'The bride's sister, right?' he said with a smile.

'Uh yes,' I replied, blushing at the direct way he looked at me.

'Are you enjoying the wedding, Ma'am?' he asked.

'Shobha,' I said, 'call me Shobha. I am too young to be called Ma'am.'

'Okay,' he grinned.

'In case you are wondering about the waiter's uniform, I'm in charge of the catering, it's my company,' he said, a constant smile on his face.

'The food is excellent,' I said, looking at my plate on the ground; too embarrassed now to pick it up.

'Well, it doesn't look as if you have tried it all,' he said sceptically, looking at my plate.

'Can I show you around the buffet?' he offered.

Just as I was going to accept his offer, Charu rushed up to me.

'Shobha, you're missing the bidai!'

Finally, everything was over. I'm not sure that I felt anything except sheer exhaustion. Even though I had felt some tingling emotions during the bidai, I couldn't muster up any tears because I had just been too tired. Though I had enjoyed it all, I was glad that this week was finally over. Just as I was about to set out to find a car that was headed home, out of the shadows emerged Harshad, now casually dressed in T-shirt, jeans and sneakers. He gave me a wide smile and I noticed again how good-looking he was. Without saying anything to me, he handed me my purse.

'You left this at the buffet.'

'Oh, thank you!'

I heard someone calling my name in the distance.

'I...I'd better go,' I said, and before he could say bye, I quickly walked away.

I couldn't stop thinking about him. During tuitions, I found myself lost in a reverie thinking of his grey-green eyes and his dashing smile. In college, the back of every nice-looking boy became Harshad's. I was constantly cooking up little fantasy stories in my mind. This was *so* unlike my normal behaviour! What had come over me? I tried to banish all thoughts of Harshad. I had so much to do, right now was not the time for love.

A few days after the wedding, I finally got around

to organizing my room which was still overflowing with wedding clothes. I emptied the purse I had carried at the wedding and I found a small piece of paper stuck in one corner.

> *Shobha,*
> *It was a pleasure to meet you. You personify your name. I would love to see you again. Please do call me if you like. My number is 80798173038.*
> *Harshad*

The note took me by surprise (and delight) and that night I went to bed with the note tucked underneath my pillow. I knew it wasn't a good idea meeting him. I hardly knew him, but I liked him so much. What if I liked him even *more* after I met him, what would happen then? I couldn't afford to get involved right now. I wanted to top in my engineering college, get a good job, leave this town before my parents married me off to some loser. Though I resisted for a full twenty hours, I just couldn't stop myself and I finally SMSed him, and that was the beginning of the end.

We fell in love faster than I could even say the word. Though I had a busy schedule, with college, CAT classes, and tuitions, I always found a way to see him. Our meeting place was the Ganesha temple, right between my house and where I went for my tuitions. I would cycle there and meet him outside. We always went in, prayed, and then got a cup of tea, a samosa, or many a time just walked around. In the maddening crowds that thronged the temple, no one noticed a couple like Harshad and me, which was a good thing, because if they did, and if they recognized me, then, there would be trouble.

I was also lucky that Papa was so busy these days—he was running for a position in the village panchayat—that he hardly noticed my presence or absence. In the one five-minute interaction I had had with him last week, he told me that he was looking for a suitable match for me. He expected quite a different reaction from the one he got: I looked at him seriously and told him that I wanted to get a job or go to a business school. Papa just scoffed when I told him this.

'A woman's place is in her husband's house, not in some office.'

When he saw my face fall, he tried to placate me.

'We will find a businessman for you, so maybe you can work in his office. You are a smart girl.'

Harshad stood firmly by my side during that stressful time of my life: on-campus placements, the CAT exams and the ensuing results. I had applied for several jobs in Delhi and Chandigarh, but I hadn't told my parents. Harshad and I had decided that he would follow me wherever I went. He reassured me that the catering business everywhere was flourishing and he could easily find a job anywhere.

Even before the CAT results came in, I got an offer from a leading IT company in Delhi. I was happy, I had so longed for this. But strangely, more than anything else, I felt nervous and scared. I had an uncomfortable gut feeling my life was about to change.

While I received good news, Papa got some bad news.

He had lost the elections and could not secure a place in the panchayat, something which I knew he had wanted badly for a long time. His loss put him into a bad mood and he was on the edge all the time.

In what was a terrible miscalculation, I shared the news of my job offer with Papa. He took my offer letter, which I had brought to show him, taking a few minutes to read the English, then told me with anger suffusing his face.

'It's because of girls like you, girls who run around town with *these* ideas in their heads,' he said shaking the paper, 'that I lost the election.'

He then ripped the paper violently into bits and threw them at me, asking me to get out of the house.

I left with tears in my eyes, and rode straight to the Ganesha temple, the only place that I could think of. I tried calling Harshad, but his phone was unreachable. I sat on the cold, marble floor of the temple, amongst the crowd of devotees, my head between my knees, as I alternated between crying and praying. In that deep moment of sadness, there was only one spark of hope, and as I prayed, that spark was fanned into a fire. There was only one way out now. I had to leave Rohtak, this was no place for me anymore. There was nothing left here for me since Namrata Di had got married; nobody except Harshad, and he too was eager to leave, to spread his wings, and to breathe. If it were up to me, I would have preferred to marry Harshad with my family by my side, but I knew that they would never agree. Harshad was from a lower caste than I was; he was from the Urmi caste, while I was a Yadav. According to Papa, inter-caste marriage was the gravest sin that a person could commit, and it was punishable only by death. Though I didn't want to think about it, I knew that there would be terrible consequences if I even brought up Harshad's name. And so I thought hard about what I (we) had to do next.

We planned it carefully. We would meet at the bus station at midnight, take the last bus to Delhi where we would take refuge with the Love Commandos, a voluntary organization which helps and protects couples in love. Harshad had spoken to Sanjoyji, the chairman of the organization, who had urged us to leave as soon as we could. He told Harshad that he would help us get married immediately, and then we could bide our time in their protection till Harshad found a job, and I started mine.

It was cold and wet that right. As the hour of our escape grew near, I felt excited and energized rather than scared or nervous. I knew it was the right decision, and though I would miss my parents and family, especially Di, I hoped that they would eventually come around and would accept Harshad into our family. For the moment, though, I needed to take control of my life. I knew that if I stayed at home, they would soon find a boy and get me married off, just as they had done to Namrata Di, and what would happen then, to Harshad and me?

I packed a few clothes, some of my favourite and precious items—a gold chain, a pair of earrings, a bangle, some payals. Also, a nice sari to wear for my wedding the next day, and a few basics that I would need. I lay in bed in the small room that I had shared with Di till she got married and went away, with many thoughts crossing my mind. It was the last night that I would spend in this room, in this house, maybe even in this town. Who knew if I would see my family again, or any of the people I had known for two decades? My life was about to change, and I didn't know what direction it would take; but at least Harshad, the man I loved more than anybody else in the world, would be by my side. I looked at my watch every few minutes, waiting anxiously till it was 11 p.m. I sneaked out without any trouble at all, making sure to give Jojo, our dog, some biscuits so that he would keep quiet. I slipped noiselessly out of the gate and made my way to the bus station where Harshad would be waiting for me.

I saw him calm and composed with that big smile on his face, and all my fears dissipated. I knew that everything was going to be fine. We stood at a distance from each other so as not to draw any attention to ourselves. When we boarded the bus, we saw that there were only ten passengers including us—five men and two women with a small child—no one who might pose any danger to us. After thirty minutes on the road, Harshad and I decided to sit together. We were fast asleep, leaning against each other's shoulder when we were rudely awakened by the stopping of the bus. I was filled with an overwhelming sense of fear.

We were all dragged out of our seats onto the road. There was a group of men with torches in their hands obstructing the bus. At first, I thought they were highway

robbers but then I saw people in the crowd whom I knew—
men whom I had called Uncle, who had come to my house,
to whom I had served tea and water. I relaxed a little until
I saw Tushar Bhaiyya wearing a turban as he had done on
his wedding day, except that this one was black.

'Bhaiyya,' I asked, 'what's going on?' but he only
glowered at me and growled, 'Don't call me Bhaiyya! How
can I possibly be related to a girl like you?' Before I could
reply, someone threw a shawl over my head and tied it
firmly around my neck. I was too surprised to scream,
even to whimper. I heard Harshad protesting before his
voice became muffled, and then two men took me by the
arm and dragged me in the direction of the forest.

Charu

Shobha and Harshad's murder or 'suicide' as the newspapers
called it, left me in a tizzy. Though it had taken me time
to comprehend fully the gravity of the situation, reality
had finally sunk in. Ever since I was a little girl, I had
known about Papa, Bhaiyya and the panchayat, but I had
turned a blind eye to their activities. Over the past few
years, it had become more and more difficult to ignore
them—the beatings, the burnings and the deaths—which
had become extreme. When Papa and Bhaiyya took out their
black turbans, I knew that something bad was going to
happen; but I had never once imagined that they would be
heartless enough to attack their own family. It was Namrata
Bhabhi who bore the brunt of it; she suspected what I knew

but, like me, she knew too that it was best to ignore it, to lie even to herself that none of it existed.

After the death of the sister whom she had loved so much, Bhabhi became just a shadow of her former self. She stopped laughing, she stopped talking, she didn't even cry. She looked at Bhaiyya with fear, and while she performed all the duties of a wife, daughter-in-law and a bhabhi, I could see from her eyes that there was no spirit left in her.

I had loved Sameer since the first day that I laid my eyes on him in tuition classes. We were both doing badly in English, and unless we passed in the subject, we would not get our college degree. I didn't care much for myself, but Papa did. He told me that these days, no decent boy would marry a girl without a degree; all boys from rich families wanted educated girls. And so, Bhaiyya enrolled me in Mr Pal's English Coaching Centre (PECC), in which I had no interest. However, I knew that the fees were high, so I only attended out of guilt. It was there that I met Sameer. It took him longer to love me, but I waited for it to happen, because I was convinced, deep in my heart that we were meant to be together. I religiously attended the classes, dressing carefully each time, even managing to improve my English significantly although I went only to see Sameer.

After he asked me out to coffee the first time, there was no going back. It just felt so correct and so natural, and we got along. He knew, as I did, that we were meant to spend the rest of our lives together. Everything happened quickly, I don't know how. I had never been so happy in anyone else's company in my entire life.

In the heady happiness of love, I didn't think of anything—not of Papa, or of Bhaiyya, or of those black turbans. Not even of the most important fact that Sameer and I came from different castes and that we could never marry, not under the auspices of our family and community at least. What the khap panchayat hated the most, more than anything else, was when lovers married out of the caste—that was when the most violent activities took place. I had seen blood-soaked clothes being burnt in the field, the guns and the knives and the looks of brutal satisfaction on their faces after they had 'punished' offending couples. But by the time Sameer and I thought about marriage, we were already so deeply in love that we couldn't imagine spending a lifetime away from each other.

To most people, I was a simple, good-natured, plain-faced girl. 'Sweet', they would call me. I didn't get into trouble, nor did I cause it. I minded my own business, lived according to my parents' wishes and closed my eyes to the awful things which happened around me. But being with Sameer had awakened something in me. I was no longer the silly or sweet or simple girl that they—and even I—thought I was. I was now capable of things if I put my mind to them, and Shobha's death had given me courage.

I knew that the only way for me to live my life as I wanted was to leave Rohtak, otherwise I would be killed like Shobha for daring to love. Running away was a dangerous and foolhardy option. Shobha had tried it, and had been murdered. I had seen what Papa and Bhaiyya, along with the khap panchayat, were capable of doing, and they would not hesitate to kill their daughter in the name of honour. I had to find another way, because desperate problems call for drastic measures.

They all loved my chikoo ka halwa, so, that's where I started. Sameer, though initially scared, agreed to cooperate after I told him about the meetings, the murders, and the burnings. Sameer got the poison: a tasteless snake venom that was the colour of dirt. I spent the whole day cooking the halwa: dicing the chikoos, soaking them in honey with just a dash of cinnamon, vanilla and snake venom, and finally mixing in the sugar and wheat before slow-cooking it all together.

I didn't feel anything at all—not when I cooked the halwa, or when I served it or while I watched them spoon it into their mouths with relish. The only time that I felt a tinge of sadness was when I saw the pregnant Namrata Di spoon a tiny bit into her mouth. She didn't deserve it, not the way the rest of them did; but there was no way at all to avoid it.

Daulat Singh

Something was fishy. I knew it when I entered that house. All four bodies lay on the floor with gashes on the throats. The girl was sobbing in one corner, her face covered with her shawl. Prima facie, it was clear—just as the girl had said—a robber had come in the middle of the night, stolen valuables, slit their throats, laid out the bodies in the living room and then escaped. She was a primary witness; she had seen and heard him do it all, but was lucky to have been hiding underneath the bed. However, years of experience told me that something just wasn't right. The way the bodies were laid out, neatly in a row, the careful linear cut of the gashes, done by an unsteady hand, that's not how it usually happened, not in a hit-and-run robbery case, which this appeared to be. Also, the motive was unclear. The family wasn't known to be rich, why then would they be targeted? And the girl...though she seemed innocent enough, there was something shifty about her eyes, something behind the tears that I noticed almost immediately; there was something about her that was not convincing.

The more I investigated the case, the more disturbing it seemed. Ever since I had been posted in Rohtak, things had gone from bad to worse—murders disguised as suicides, deaths cloaked in deceit. As Rohtak modernized, with more colleges, schools, industries and malls, the khap panchayats, instead of getting diluted, had only become more powerful. Though there were no official witnesses, I had heard stories of the black turbans, the sudden disappearances and the honour killings. I knew that Yashwant Hooda and his son Tushar were staunch members of the panchayat and that their daughter-in-law's sister had reportedly committed suicide with her boyfriend close to the Delhi border. There were reports too of Charu, the last remaining member of the family, and a boy who had been hanging around with her.

I couldn't put it all together. Who would have executed the cold-blooded murders of the Hooda family and why?

It was an old habit of mine to revisit the scene of the crime in whichever case I was investigating. The Hooda household had been sealed, and everything remained exactly as on the day of the crime. Though she had resisted, we even made sure that Charu could not visit the site. I was convinced that the clues were here somewhere, if I looked hard enough, but in this particular case, I was at my wits' end.

Something made me go into the kitchen; maybe it was the stench of rotting food, or my investigator's nose. Everything was neat and clean, in place, though a few used dishes were piled up in the sink. Exactly the way things had been on the night of the crime. As I walked about, I suddenly noticed the colour of the dishes: the white of the ceramic bowls were stained with a brilliant, deep blue, like a peacock's feather. It was the most curious thing I had seen. I had never seen any food of this particular colour. What could it possibly be? Doubt seared my mind. These days, with all the strange processed things around, who knew what people consumed? I brought the bowl close to my nose and sniffed the bowl. What was that smell— discreet but foul, not the smell of rot, but of something else that I couldn't figure out.

Though I expected nothing at all, I sent one of the bowls to the lab. I had a habit, which irritated many of my colleagues, of testing everything. I told them that it was the chemistry student in me that did this jugaad.

Much to my surprise, the lab report showed traces of snake venom. I called for an autopsy immediately, on the day before the bodies were to be cremated. The autopsy confirmed that the entire Hooda family had been poisoned. The only suspects were Charu and the servants. Though most of my colleagues thought it was cruel of me to question the young girl—after all, her entire family had been killed—I followed my instinct as a good cop always does, and I knew right away that something was amiss. We tracked her movements for a few days, and quickly discovered that she had a boyfriend, a young boy whom she frequently met.

He broke down the minute we approached him, and within the hour he had told us the entire story. The girl, it turned out, was far more ruthless than the boy. They were both under eighteen, so they were treated as juveniles and, when convicted, were sent to juvenile correction centres. I felt sympathy for the boy. Love had ruined his life. As for the girl, I was convinced that she had a criminal mind and I hoped, though I strongly doubted, that a few years in a correction centre would teach her a lesson. In my early days as a cop I had thought differently, but now experience had taught me that hardened criminal minds, minds that were capable of murdering their entire family, could rarely be corrected. Once a criminal, always a criminal.

ॐ

Double MMS

'Yes, Ma, I've eaten,' laughed Priya into the phone. 'I've got to go to college now, okay? I'll call you in the evening. Bye!' said Priya as she hung up and walked towards her cupboard, deciding what to wear.

As she sat in the Mumbai local train on her way to college, Priya could still scarcely believe it. Here she was in the sparkling city of Mumbai! The city of dreams, the city that never sleeps—so far removed from her conservative hometown of Kanpur.

Just a month ago, Priya, who was barely seventeen, had come to Mumbai to study Mass Communications at Mumbai University. The city had taken her by surprise. Here, everyone seemed to be in a hurry; no one had the time to stop and chat, girls smoked openly, wore skimpy shorts and hung out with guys, and nobody even batted an eyelid. Raised in a traditional middle class family, initially, this had been a shock to Priya. She could never imagine this happening back home, where she went to a convent school, wore salwar-kameezes only, and never spoke to boys.

Her parents had been reluctant to send her to Mumbai, but this was a great opportunity for Priya—her course was a prestigious one which they knew would open plenty of doors—and at the end of the day, her parents did want the best for her.

After a morning of lectures, Priya headed to the café for some chai. The canteen was buzzing with some students taking a break between lectures and others missing classes. Coming from a disciplined convent school, the latter was out of the question for Priya, but she knew that many of her classmates did it quite brazenly. She ordered a chai and opened a book she had borrowed from the library. She had barely begun reading when her friend Swati walked up to her table.

'Hey Priya, how's it going?' asked Swati as she sat down at the table with a plate of bhel-puri.

'Just the usual,' groaned Priya. 'A morning of boring lectures.'

'Arre, don't worry! You'll get used to it,' Swati smiled at her. 'By the way, I've got some news that'll cheer you up.'

'Really? What?' asked Priya eagerly, taking a sip of her chai.

'The annual college fashion show!' Swati exclaimed. 'It's the most awesome event in college—a magical evening of dancing, partying. It's great!'

'When is it happening?' asked Priya, enthusiastically.

'Next Friday, and I just can't wait!' chimed Swati excitedly.

Later that night in her room Priya couldn't stop thinking

about the fashion show. All this was so alien and yet so exciting at the same time. She could never imagine an event like this happening back at her school, where the most-looked-forward-to event was the boring annual Christmas Carnival. There was no way the stern and unsmiling nuns who ran the school would give permission for something as 'scandalous' as a fashion show! Mumbai was different, Mumbai was new. Mumbai was a wide-open blue sky where Priya was itching to stretch her wings.

On the evening of the fashion show, Priya chose her outfit carefully. She was determined to look right and fit into the crowd, something that she hadn't managed to do so far. She felt totally out of place with her uniform of short kurtas (which her mother had got the tailor to stitch in ten different colours) and jeans. She chose her favourite pair of jeans that was tighter than the others and showed off her lean frame, and a pink floral top she usually reserved for special occasions. She carefully lined her eyes with kohl, straightened her hair and wore a pair of delicate earrings. She thought she looked fine, but that feeling lasted only until she reached the fashion show venue. Everyone there was far better dressed than she was. The girls wore short strappy dresses, impossibly high heels in striking colours and so much make-up that they looked like movie stars. They carried themselves with total confidence and strutted about proudly. Even the slightly overweight girls wore dresses with the highest hemlines and carried them off well. Looking around, Priya began to feel underdressed— her hair felt frizzy and her make-up incomplete. She was still fretting over the way she looked when Swati grabbed her by the arm and led her to the ramp where the fashion show was about to begin.

Once it began, everyone's eyes were on the ramp, down which, one after the other, some of the best-looking and stylish girls and boys on the campus started walking. But there was one girl who instantly caught her eye.

'That's Renuka,' whispered Swati, 'she's doing her post-grad and she's one of the hottest girls on campus.'

The minute Renuka stepped on the ramp, the audience erupted into applause. Priya couldn't help but notice the way the guys were whistling at her and the envious looks the girls were giving her. She was wearing one of the prettiest dresses Priya had ever seen—the kind of dress Priya had seen only on models in magazines. But then, Renuka was no less than a model herself. She was tall, had long cascading curly hair, a flawless skin, a dimpled smile and never-ending long legs.

Soon after the fashion show, the dancing began and, as was to be expected, Renuka was the centre of attention on the dance floor. She had all the right dance moves—subtle yet sexy. Priya watched it all glumly from the sidelines. She wasn't much of a dancer, and she certainly could not go on the dance floor in the clothes she was wearing. Swati walked up to where Priya was sitting and handed her a Coke.

'She's just so stunning, isn't she?' said Swati, looking at Renuka. 'No wonder she's the star at all the college fashion shows.'

'Hmm...' nodded Priya, who was at a loss for words as

she stared at the beautiful Renuka. 'Well, that's the thing with Renuka, she's popular and she knows it,' laughed Swati, draining her Coke and collecting her handbag to leave.

That night, as Priya tried to finish her homework, her mind kept returning to the fashion show and to Renuka. How nice to be the most admired and envied girl on campus! But, this was a position that Priya too had held not so long ago.

Back in Kanpur, Priya had been one of the most admired students in her school. Not only was she the Head Girl, but she was also a topper academically and in extra-curricular activities. She was a favourite with all her teachers, who constantly praised her and held her up as a role model. Priya was competitive and was used to being the centre of attention and she wasn't going to let go of that just because she was new in the city.

She didn't sleep much that night. She spent the better part of the night burning with resentment and envy. She couldn't stand the thought of someone else getting more attention than her. She knew that if she tried she could be as popular as Renuka, if not more. She had to get noticed, that was all; and from there, it would be an easy ride. Priya knew that the path towards stardom might not be straightforward, and that there may be twists and turns on the way. But then again, Priya knew how to deal with that. With a smile on her face, she remembered locking her competitor in the bathroom during a debate competition; she remembered tripping her rival before the 400-metre race so that she could win the best athlete award; she remembered stealing question papers from the teachers' room. That night, a determined Priya made up her mind that she was going to be the most popular girl on campus and she was prepared to do anything to achieve it.

'Priya, you must be crazy!' laughed Swati when she told her about her goal. 'This isn't Kanpur, you know. This is Mumbai! Catching and holding people's attention here isn't as easy as you think,' laughed Swati. 'Moreover, you've come here to study, Priya; just focus on that.'

It was easy enough for Swati to say that, thought Priya. After all, Swati was overweight, uncool, and did not want anything more out of life than to read silly romance novels. Priya wanted a lot more .

'Renuka is Renuka,' shrugged Swati. 'She's so popular already; just forget it, Priya,' said Swati, walking away.

Priya remained silent. What would Swati know?

Priya was determined. She wouldn't let Renuka's popularity last for long. It was her turn now and Renuka would have to step back. Sitting on her bed that evening, her eyes scanned the medals and trophies lined up against her wall: 'Student of the Year' two times in a row, gold medals won for extra-curricular activities every academic year. She may be a small town girl, but Priya had tasted popularity and success on her own and was hungry for more. The next day, as she sat studying in the library, Swati approached her with a grin on her face.

'What's with that big smile?' laughed Priya.

'Well, I've got a message for you,' beamed Swati.

'From whom?' probed Priya.

'From Mayank,' Swati smiled naughtily.

'Who's Mayank?' Priya frowned.

'Arre, he's Renuka's younger brother,' said Swati. 'How could you not have heard of him? Everyone keeps talking about him on campus.'

That was when it dawned upon Priya. No wonder the name had sounded familiar. Just the other day, she had overheard two girls in her class talking about Mayank and giggling.

'He really likes you, Priya,' smiled Swati excitedly. 'He's seen you with me in the canteen a couple of times and thinks you're cute.'

'He wanted me to tell you how he felt,' continued Swati. 'So? What do you think?'

A smile began to play on Priya's lips. This was her chance. She could be the girlfriend of one of the most popular guys on campus, why not?

Soon, Priya and Mayank began dating. But little did he know that she was exploiting his feelings for her own selfish pursuit. Each time they went out on a date, she clicked numerous selfies of them together which she posted on Facebook. Their pictures soon began to get numerous likes and comments from their college friends.

Priya was thrilled to be the centre of attention finally. Dating one of the most popular guys in college certainly had its perks—she hung out with some of the coolest students on campus, was invited to the right parties, and both the boys and the girls began to notice her and say hello to her in the corridors.

Even though Mayank was uncomfortable with it, Priya would indulge in PDA—public display of affection—and she insisted on hugging him, nuzzling his neck and pecking him on the cheek, ensuring that there were enough people around to see them. One day in the college canteen, having already seen a few of their class guys sitting at the next table, Priya grabbed Mayank's face and kissed him on the cheek. They erupted in hoots and shrieks. 'Just look at them, man, all over each other! Get a room, you two!' they laughed.

Mayank pushed Priya away. 'Priya, what the hell do you think you're doing?' he demanded. He was red in the face and seething with anger. Before she could say anything, he stormed out of the canteen.

After a few days of no communication, Priya received a phone call from Mayank.

'Hey, Priya, listen. I've been thinking and I've realized that I was too harsh on you. I mean it was just a kiss and who cares what those stupid guys said?' Mayank apologized.

Priya was surprised. She had been feeling rotten for the past couple of days, and had wondered whether she had lost Mayank because of her silly, attention-seeking behaviour.

'How about coming over to my place and talking this over?' Mayank suggested.

'Oh, Mayank. I'm so sorry about everything,' cooed Priya as she gave Mayank a hug, and cuddled up against him.

Mayank too was genuinely happy to see his girlfriend

after the short break.

'How about some coffee?' offered Mayank.

'We can have coffee later,' smiled Priya. 'First, I have a surprise for you.'

Little did Mayank know what Priya had in mind. Her obsession with being popular had consumed her completely, and she didn't mind stooping to any level to achieve fame. With her phone camera strategically placed in her half-open purse, Priya began performing a striptease in front of Mayank. She seductively shed one item of clothing after another, till she was completely naked. He stared at her aghast, not sure how to feel about it. His mind felt one thing, his heart felt another, while his groin something completely different.

Later in the evening, Priya made an MMS out of the recording of her striptease and circulated it in college. She knew that she would soon be the topic of gossip on campus. But Priya didn't care. For her, any publicity was good publicity.

By the time Priya reached college the next day, she had become a celebrity of sorts. Suddenly everyone on campus knew her. While the girls sympathized with her, the guys couldn't stop staring at her. Priya was the talk of the campus—just what she wanted.

In the meantime, Mayank found out what had happened and was desperately trying to call Priya, but she avoided his calls. High on the attention and sympathy that she was getting, she didn't anticipate the quick succession of events that would follow.

It was not long before Priya's parents found out about the scandal. Assuming their daughter was an innocent victim of Mayank's lust, they filed a police case. Mayank, the obvious perpetrator, was called in for questioning, but though he kept denying his involvement in the MMS, the police harassment didn't end quickly.

Following the MMS scandal and the continuing police interrogation, Mayank stopped going to college. Deeply shocked and distressed, he still couldn't accept what Priya had done. His phone rang constantly, his classmates kept calling, curious to get a low-down on what had happened.

Mayank's gaunt face was dark with stubble and he looked haggard. He barely ate and couldn't sleep at night. Dark rings appeared under his eyes and he sat brooding in his room most of the day. He was at his wits' end; confused and perturbed, he didn't know what to do. One night, as he sat in his room, glum and depressed, his father walked in. Mayank came from an influential family. His father was a successful businessman, well-known in Mumbai, and it was getting difficult for him to answer people's questions about his son's involvement in the MMS scandal.

'Son, I know this is a difficult time for you, but I need you to be honest with me. Did you have anything to do with that MMS?' his father gently questioned.

'Absolutely not, Papa!' said Mayank, a frown creasing his forehead. 'My feelings for Priya were real and I thought she felt the same way about me. I just can't *believe* all this,' he cried.

'If that is the truth, then I will ensure that Sharma

Sahab sorts out this mess,' asserted Mayank's father. 'Don't worry, beta. No matter what happens, we will always be with you and support you. Keep faith,' said his father, patting his arm.

Luckily for Mayank, his father's lawyer had contacts in the right places. It wasn't long before he was let off by the police.

In the meantime, Priya was enjoying all the attention and sympathy she was getting from her classmates, and she continued to play the innocent victim and abused heroine. She spread stories of how Mayank had used her to satisfy his lust and how she could not face her parents, nor go back to Kanpur because of him.

One evening, a few days later, Swati dropped by at Priya's place.

'Hey,' Swati enveloped Priya in a warm hug. 'You okay?' she asked, genuinely concerned.

'Not really,' mumbled Priya, putting on a miserable expression.

'In that case I have just the thing to cheer you up!' smiled Swati, opening her bag, and pulling out a bottle of peach flavoured vodka and some soda.

Priya was a bit taken aback. She had never had a drink before. Her father was a teetotaller, and she had never seen a bottle of alcohol up close before; but she wasn't going to let Swati know that. She decided to play along.

She couldn't decide whether she liked the drink or not it was pretty strong, but it also had a nice peachy flavour. She liked the way the drink was making her feel—warm, tingly, relaxed and a bit woozy, and she began to gulp it down. It wasn't long before the alcohol began to have an effect on her; she slurred her words and giggled uncontrollably without reason.

'I can't tell you how wonderful these last few days have been! I've been getting so much attention and I'm feeling on top of the world,' sighed Priya in a drunken stupor.

'Priya, are you okay?' Swati was getting concerned. 'Maybe you should go a little slow with your drink. Here, have some water.' Swati offered her a glass.

Swati, on the other hand, had a good control over her drink. Her father was in the army and she had secretly been raiding his liquor cabinet since she was fourteen. Her parents, of course had no idea of her little habit.

'Oh, no!' slurred Priya, waving away the glass of water. 'I'm fine. In fact I think I'll have another drink,' said Priya, lurching towards the bottle.

Swati remained silent and sipped her drink. By then, the alcohol had a complete hold over Priya and she spilled out whatever she had been holding back.

'You know, Swati, I was the *most* popular girl in my school,' began Priya. 'I topped my class every year...even topped the school in my board exams. Evvvveryoooone knew me. My teachers *loooved* me and my parents were sooooo proud of me.

'Then I came to *Mumbai* and I began to feel lost. No one knew me...I was *just* an ordinary, pathetic loser from a small town.

'And that Renuka...*everyone* loves her, everyone admires

her! What's so special about her, huh? I'm sooooo much better than that...that Little Miss Popular. You watch, Swati, I'll sooooon be more popular than her.

'Once enough people have seen that MMS, they'll forget who Renuka was, it'll be me about whom everyone will be talking. Me...Priya, everyone will know who *I* am!' Priya spluttered in a drunken haze.

'Priya, what do you mean? I don't understand. What about the MMS?' Swati asked, confused. 'Mayank made that MMS, right? You've been so upset since then.'

Priya howled with laughter. 'Mayank is too seedha-saadha. It was I who made that video and *I* who circulated it. Clever of me, no?' Priya laughed devilishly.

Swati was stunned, and she stared aghast at the drunk Priya.

Finally she found words. 'Why would you do something so sick, Priya?' demanded Swati.

'I want to be *popular*, okaaaay, just like Renuka! I want everyone in college to know who *I* am,' cried Priya gleefully.

'I can't believe that you would stoop so low,' cried Swati in disbelief. She had known that Priya hankered after popularity, but this...this was a whole new ballgame.

'You're totally self-obsessed!' Swati yelled. 'I'm ashamed to have ever called you my friend,' cried Swati as she stormed out.

Feeling upset and guilty that her friend Mayank—whom she herself had introduced to Priya—had been framed for something that he had not done, Swati immediately contacted the police and told them what had really happened.

The police called Priya in for questioning. The interrogation was tough. She was asked many questions, she was cross-questioned, and she had to face a team of six senior cops. Priya broke down under the stress and the pressure, and soon gave in. She told the police the truth and took back her charges. She apologized to Mayank and his family. She thought she was off the hook, but little did she know that she had messed with the wrong person.

Renuka was seething with rage. She couldn't believe that Priya had had the audacity to put her family through such misery for no fault of her brother. It pained her to see the distress Mayank was going through: he was no longer the brother she had known. He had lost weight, he hardly smiled, and to make things worse, he had quit college. She wondered if and when he would ever go back to being the old Mayank.

She was also concerned about her father, a heart patient. She worried that all this anxiety might just bring on a second heart attack. Her mother did not say much, but her face betrayed her grief and anguish.

Renuka was further enraged when she found out that the police had let Priya off the hook so easily, with a mere warning. Who did that chit of a girl think she was, anyway? And if the police weren't going to do anything to punish Priya, then she would; she would teach her a lesson she would never forget. Renuka was consumed with the desire to avenge the torture her family had been put through. Soon she had a plan ready.

The next day, while Priya was sitting in the canteen,

two of Renuka's friends came up to her.

'Hey, Priya! We're going for fashion show rehearsals. Wanna come? We thought that maybe you could take part as well. You do have a really good figure.'

Priya was thrilled. This was her dream come true! A part in the annual fashion show? What more could she ask for? She readily agreed, and went with them in the car to pick up Renuka and two other girls. She felt fine till she noticed that the car was on the freeway, headed towards Chembur. She wondered where they were going, and began to feel ill at ease, but she couldn't muster up the courage to ask.

Things happened so quickly thereafter that Priya barely remembers them. The car stopped, the five girls, including Renuka, covered their faces with scarves and gagged her to muffle her screams. Before she could take in what was happening, they pinned her down to the car seat and started tearing off her clothes. Priya panicked and tried to fight them off; she scratched and kicked but she was outnumbered. She was desperate and shouted for help but the music had been turned on really loud and her cries remained inside the car. She felt them fondling her private parts, squeezing her bare breasts, touching her vagina, laughing out cruelly and loudly as they did.

Before she could make sense of what had happened, Priya was thrown out of the car, naked. Renuka and her friends went to a cyber café and uploaded the video they had taken, thinking no one would be able to trace them.

Priya was shaken, but had the presence of mind to

report the matter to the police immediately. Given Priya's previous false accusation, the police were initially hesitant to believe her the second time around; but upon hearing the full story, and seeing the state she was in when she was found, they agreed. The police nabbed Renuka and her allies and after conducting an investigation, all five students involved in Priya's molestation were charge-sheeted and put into jail.

Unfortunately for Renuka, her case hasn't yet come to an end, nor has the shame and pain through which her family has gone because of her. Priya learnt a lesson the hard way when she was molested and when the second case became public and hit the newspapers. She was so traumatized that she had to leave Mumbai and return to Kanpur where she is undergoing psychological treatment. Her story followed her to Kanpur from where, eventually, she and her family were driven out by media attention.

∽

Binoy and Pari

One, two, three, four, five, six...Binoy would count while the other children hid in the surrounding field. He would open his eyes and look only for Pari. Even if it took him a while, even though he spotted the others, he would persevere until he found her. He ruined the game for everyone else, but it was the only way that he ever played.

The game was stuck in Pari's head even now, and she told me with a smile that, after every game of hide-and-seek, the kids would ignore Binoy for a few days. Not Pari. For her, Binoy was always priority and she would run to him whenever he called out to her.

It's not that I saw her life unfold from the very beginning, but because she told me so much about it that I felt like I had. She is my roommate at St Xavier's College in Mumbai, and we are best friends. It hadn't begun like that. We didn't become friends easily. We were as different as chalk and cheese—she was beautiful, with her bronzed skin, cascading curls, bright eyes and effervescent smile, while I was short, stocky, nervous everywhere except on stage, and I had frizzy hair that could never be tamed. But our commonalities brought us together: we were both from small towns, she from Shillong and I from Mysore; we were both drama students (though Pari was a star and I wasn't); and more than anything else, we both wanted to make something of ourselves. Neither of us wanted what most of the other girls in our college wanted: to get married, have a few children and then spend the rest of their lives looking after children and husbands. Pari and I were dreamers, and we both felt that here in Mumbai, the world was our oyster.

I wasn't the only one who shared a dream with Pari. Before me there was Binoy, who had shared her dream of moving out of the small town of Shillong. Binoy and she were opposites. She was interested in art and dramatics while he was a mathematics wiz. Theatre was her passion while numbers was what he lived for. She was social, while he only enjoyed the company of one human being—her. Yet, they were best friends; they had been since they were five, and though they were so different, she felt that he was the only one who really understood her.

∽

'It is only August, *why* do you have to prepare now for the December play?' Binoy grumbled.

'If I don't prove to the teachers that I can do this play, then I won't get the chance at the end of the year. I *need* to get into St Xavier's, Mumbai, and I *need* this gig...you *know* that all my whole life I've wanted to go to that college,'

Pari reminded him.

'But one movie won't make any difference,' grumbled Binoy.

'Binoy, you're being unfair. You've let NOTHING interfere with your IIT coaching. I'm sure you'll get your dream college, IIT-Delhi. Remember, this is *our* chance to get out of this small town and do something big for ourselves. I need to work hard,' Pari reasoned.

'I don't want to be in Delhi while you're in Mumbai,' he said, looking down at his shoes, a shadow crossing his face.

'Binoy! Shouldn't we be thinking of our careers and lives instead of our friendship? We *have* to focus on our futures.'

Pari realized that she had inadvertently upset Binoy, but she thought that maybe it was because he was just as nervous about moving to an unknown city as she was. But she knew that life was more than Shillong, and even though her friendship with Binoy was precious, she wouldn't let it get in the way of her dreams.

The winter months passed, and soon Shillong burst into spring, putting everyone in good spirits. The end of the school year was approaching, and Pari couldn't contain her joy. Rehearsals for the annual school play had begun, exams were around the corner, and soon she would be out of here, and off to college. But before all that she had a major hurdle to clear: she *had* to do well in her exams. She had to score more than 90 per cent if she wanted to enter her dream college—Xavier's in Mumbai.

As it invariably happens, the exams came upon them

suddenly, and both Binoy and Pari spent the next few weeks cramming over long hours, sleeping short hours and worrying about the future. But soon they ended, and both of them were finally free.

It was during the long summer before they started college, and while they waited impatiently for their board results, that Pari began to wonder about Binoy. What would happen if they kissed? How would it feel? Could she imagine him as more than her best friend? But the more she thought about it, the more she became convinced that they should only remain friends. She just didn't feel that way about him. She loved him dearly, but it wasn't *that* sort of love. Though she had never been in love before, she was convinced that it had to feel different from this. It was around this time that she had her first doubts about Binoy. She would catch him staring at her with a strange expression on his face, but she chose to ignore it, looking away and pretending that it never happened.

Finally, after a long wait, their results came out. Binoy had done spectacularly in the JEE and Pari had scored 94 per cent. She was overwhelmed. With such a good result, she could have her pick of the lot, and that meant only Xavier's. As for Binoy, though he could have picked IIT-Delhi—the college of his dreams—he chose IIT-Mumbai so that he could be closer to Pari. She protested, telling him that he should go to Delhi, that Delhi and Mumbai were just a flight away, but he was adamant, and told her that he had changed his mind about the course that he wanted to take, and that IIT-Mumbai was better suited for it. While he was happy for Pari, and also for himself, knowing that both of them were closer to achieving their dreams, he sensed an impending change. He knew that things were bound to be different when they went to Mumbai. Here in Shillong, Pari was his, and only his, but in Mumbai she would make new friends, create a new life without him, and the thought of her doing that was devastating. As for her, she couldn't wait for her life to change. She felt as if she had always been working towards this; finally, her shackles had been broken and she was on her way.

∽

Pari took to college life immediately. She was incredibly talented and was an instant hit in DramSoc, the college drama society. Even though she wasn't as 'cool' as the local girls, she was so earnest and charming that everyone liked her. Binoy, on the other hand, hated his college and all the people there. Instead of making friends and integrating into college life, he waited for Pari's calls. Though she wanted to be there for him, his clinginess bothered her. She was trying hard to build a new life, and he was getting in her way. Moreover, she couldn't understand why he was so unhappy—IIT had been his dream, after all. His behaviour, his endless calls and the constant SMSs were troubling, and when I remarked on it, she brushed it aside, saying it was just the love and affection of a childhood friend.

Our first few months passed by in a blur. This was

Mumbai after all, and Pari and I were trying to take it all in. We were determined to have it all—good marks, good friends and good times, and in the heady pursuit of these goals, there was little or no time for the past.

Shobhit showed up in her life when she least expected it. Very appropriately, she met him at a rehearsal. He had just returned from doing a short film course in England where he had specialized in set design. Pari was assistant director (the only first-year student to get this role) and was desperately looking for talented set designers. He agreed to help her and there, on the sets of *Hamlet*, began their love story. Pari was besotted by Shobhit's South Mumbai charm, his sense of humour, the fact that he had travelled the world and that he played the guitar. He loved her childish charm, her nymph-like looks, and her perpetual earnestness. Soon, over endless hours of play practice, Shobhit and Pari became inseparable, and I knew that Pari was falling in love.

Binoy still called and visited but, much to Pari's relief, it seemed that he too had somewhat settled into IIT, and had even made a couple of friends. Just when she thought that he was finally happy in Mumbai, one afternoon, uninvited, Binoy showed up outside our hostel.

'Why do I feel like you are avoiding me? Why is it that you can't spend some more time with me?' questioned the frustrated Binoy.

'Binoy, we study in different colleges, we lead separate lives. Life is not what it used to be. Our meeting often when we live so far from each other is not practical. It was normal when we were neighbours back home, but not anymore.'

'We spent time together then, and now I'm making an effort to see each other more. What's it to you? You're not wasting your precious time, are you?'

'Binoy...' she said hesitantly, 'we had nothing else to do in Shillong. Here, my days are packed. Maybe if you focused on your studies...'

'You are changing and becoming someone else. Our friendship doesn't matter to you *at all*,' said Binoy, now on the verge of tears.

'That's so not true!' she said, trying to placate him, reaching out to hold his hand. 'I *always* said that when I came to Mumbai I would work towards changing my life. What's wrong with change? I have priorities and so should you. *Now* is the time for us to create new lives.'

'Pari...' he said softly, 'you *are* a part of the life I want to create,' said Binoy, looking at her intently.

'Binoy, don't irritate me with this silly talk. We *are* a part of each other's lives. We always will be. But we should give each other space...'

And then, after a pause, she added, 'And you shouldn't come here too often.'

'Don't tell me what to do and what not to!' he said.

With that he got up and walked away in a rage.

When she recounted the argument to me over breakfast the next day, Pari seemed deeply disturbed. She said that she wanted desperately to be there for him. She loved him, like a brother almost, but his behaviour was suffocating.

She wished he would settle into college life so he wouldn't bother her anymore. I didn't know what to say to her, it was obvious that Binoy loved her. I had told her many times that she should sit down and explain things to him gently, and tell him that she didn't love him like that. But she had chosen to ignore this crucial fact and she had arrived at her own conclusions.

∽

When we walked into Shobhit's house, sounds of jazz floated from the home theatre system into the fancy living room. I had never seen a home or an apartment like this— so modern and fancy, more like a hotel than a house! I thought back to my small home in Mysore, cramped with books and images of gods—this looked nothing like that. I could tell from the way he greeted her that he had been waiting for her to arrive, and from the minute she walked into the room, he had eyes only for her.

I am not much of a party person, and I certainly wasn't comfortable at fashionable parities such as this. I tugged self-consciously at the dowdy kurta that I was wearing, and felt out of place in my ill-fitting jeans. Pari, though, was centre stage and totally comfortable in that role. She had come a long way since her initial days in the city—from being a slightly awkward kid to being the belle of the ball. While I sat self-consciously in a corner, Shobhit and Pari spent most of the evening together, on the balcony, nursing their drinks and staring into each other's eyes.

At midnight, I called for a taxi to take us back to the

hostel and as Pari got in, Shobhit kissed her on the lips. Pari turned red—I'm not sure whether in embarrassment or happiness, but it was obvious that she was head over heels in love.

That night, all I could think of was Binoy. Pari had brought only one picture from Shillong—a small framed photograph, which she had placed on her desk, of Binoy and her as kids, smiling, their arms around each other's shoulders. The photograph, I noticed, was now covered with a thick layer of dust.

'Does Binoy know about Shobhit?' I asked her as we both lay in bed, sleep eluding us.

'I don't know how to tell him, Ruchi,' she said with a sigh. 'I like Shobhit...but Binoy... he's been a bit weird lately,' she said, clearly distressed.

'Listen, you should tell him sooner rather than later. It's better for him to know,' I said quietly.

'I don't know how he'll react, Ruchi. I can't predict his behaviour like I used to; and I'm scared too of his outbursts,' said Pari in a small voice.

∽

Pari had to face Binoy sooner than she had expected. The very next day, he showed up outside the DramSoc building after practice and convinced Pari to have lunch with him. Everything seemed to be normal. He was his old, sweet, gentle self. She regaled him with stories from her upcoming production, and he listened eagerly. He told her about college, and all the friends that he had managed to make there. All in all, lunch reminded her of the old Binoy, the Binoy from Shillong, the Binoy who was her best friend and soulmate.

As she walked him to the bus stop, he suddenly turned towards her and held her hand.

'Pari, I love you,' he said softly, squeezing her hand with so much force that it hurt.

She was taken unawares; she didn't know how to respond. But finally, after an uncomfortable silence, she said, 'I love you too...but only as a friend, like a brother.'

He looked at her stricken, his chin quivering.

'You know I've always loved you. How could you not?' he asked softly.

'I...I'm sorry if I gave you the wrong idea, Binoy. I really am. I'm in love with someone else, he's a boy from my college, my senior...we really like each other, and...and I want you to meet him.'

Binoy's eyes widened in shock. Then, he stepped towards her so that their faces were just inches apart and in a tearful voice he said to her, 'You were just using me in Shillong. You had no one there, so you kept me tagging along.'

Before she could respond, he turned around and walked away.

Pari spent that night crying in bed. I tried to comfort her, but I was at a loss. I didn't know what to say or do that would make her feel better. I didn't want to be harsh with her in her moment of weakness, but I knew that in many ways this was her own mistake. Binoy's feelings for her had been clear from the start, but she had deliberately misread them. She had refused to face the problem and solve it, and now, with Shobhit in the picture, things had gone from bad to worse.

In the days that followed, Binoy, the rejected lover, began to stalk Pari. He followed her, moped about the campus, sneaked into the library, and waited for her outside the hostel. Even in my wildest dreams, I could not have imagined this, and she too was astounded that he would go to such crazy lengths. She thought about complaining to her parents, or to his, but she didn't want to embarrass him; after all, she did love him.

At first, when he showed up outside the hostel, she tried talking to him; then she screamed at him, asking him to leave, and when he didn't listen, she just ignored him completely, no matter what he did to catch her attention.

The way things were going, disaster was bound to strike sooner or later.

One evening, after the DramSoc meeting, Binoy saw Pari walking with Shobhit down the corridor. He had been waiting outside the building with a bouquet of flowers, hoping to apologize to her for his bad behaviour. Enraged at seeing them together, he stomped towards them and grabbed her from behind. Shobhit pushed him away and told him to back off but Binoy, in a fit of anger, slapped him. He was about to hit Shobhit again, when, quivering with fear and nervous as hell, I stepped in and threatened to call the security guards. Binoy stared at all of us and then walked away, swearing at us. Pari had just stood on the sidelines watching all this, and even though I advised her to, she dismissed my idea of getting Binoy's parents involved. For some reason, she thought that he would see reason, and would eventually revert to being the best friend whom she had known all her life.

Binoy didn't come to our college for a week and Pari relaxed, beginning to believe that maybe things would be normal. But just a few days later, he followed Shobhit who was riding a bike and attacked him from behind, so that he fell off his bike and onto a busy road. He could easily have been run over by a car or a truck, but fortunately, a few kind Samaritans came to his rescue and took him to a hospital. Shobhit was discharged with a few stitches and two fractured bones. He went immediately to the police station and registered a complaint against Binoy.

Pari and I didn't know any of this until Binoy's mother rang her up. Pari was shocked and disgusted at the news; she couldn't believe how her Binoy, the kind, gentle guy she had known all her life, could have done something so terrible.

She went to Shobhit and pleaded with him to withdraw the case, but he wouldn't hear of it. He insisted that a mentally disturbed person like Binoy was better off in an institution, and Pari knew there was a grain of truth in what he said. Distraught, and because Binoy's mother asked her to, she went to the police station to meet him but he refused to speak to her. She was torn between Shobhit, Binoy, and his mother, who rang Pari and implored her to remain at the police station, by his side till she arrived.

She was stuck between the devil and the deep sea—Binoy's mother had been like a mother to her, how could she avoid her request?

Binoy was in police custody for a couple of days and was then handed a restraining order around Shobhit. Binoy's mother called to tell Pari that she was taking him home to Shillong and that if the doctors deemed him stable, he would return to Mumbai. Else, he would have to go to college close to home. We had both been stunned by the awful turn of events, so the news of Binoy's coming departure came as a welcome relief to us.

Binoy had sent Pari a long email saying that he was leaving Mumbai, and that he might not come back for a long while, if at all. He wanted to meet her one last time and apologize for his behaviour. After that, he promised, he would never contact her again. He told her that it would mean the world to him, and that it would give him closure which, the doctors had said, was important in his treatment. Pari was apprehensive, but in the end she agreed to see him. I knew it was a mistake, but I went along because she insisted.

When we stepped off at the bus stop, we saw him waiting for us, standing on the flyover that spanned the busy road. He saw us walking towards him and, with his eyes on us, Binoy climbed on to the parapet of the flyover. Pari shouted at him, asking him to get down, and started running even as horns honked wildly around her and people yelled at her for pushing them out of the way. I couldn't keep up with her, and I got stuck in the crowds. And then, without a warning or a word, just before she reached him, Binoy, staring intently at her, stepped off the parapet and into the dense, moving traffic below.

∽

Scandal

'Mayaaa!' I screamed. My 4-year-old was getting on my nerves. She was running around, skidding on the floor, rumpling the carpet, breaking a vase, and almost waking up her 2-year-old sister Fareeb, who had fallen asleep. Maya scowled and ran up the staircase only to come sliding down the banister.

The servants pampered her. Maya hated me because I tried to curb her increasingly bad behaviour. But the truth was that nothing I said or did really mattered to her. She just ran to her father, who always let her have her way. Her father, my husband Rajat, lived in his own world. I know I should be grateful for him, Ma says so, but I can't be, not with what I know about him.

'Beatrice, please ensure that Maya sleeps; she has eaten her food already. Have you seen Sir today?' I asked the housekeeper.

'Sir left in the morning after Hugo arrived. I have moved Hugo's suitcases to the guest room. Sir said that he is likely to stay over...' she said, blushing. 'Sir said he expects to see you at 8 p.m. for dinner and he suggested that we have prawns sautéed in garlic and pepper, tangy crispy lamb, and chicken curry with jasmine rice for dinner,' said Beatrice.

'Quite a feast...for Hugo, of course,' I said as I turned around to leave, Beatrice staring after me.

Hugo will be in Rajat's bedroom tonight and I in mine. And 'our' bedroom will be empty, as usual. Hugo is not a good influence, and I don't like to have him around the kids, but then again, who am I to say anything? Most of the times, I feel like a prisoner in my own house.

I wanted to look pretty, yet not catch anyone's eye. These days, I never did. The sea-blue kaftan and grey tights seemed perfect for my mood. Synchronizing with my opening the door, the car stopped at the entrance to the house. 'I want to walk. It's just five minutes from here. I want fresh air, not the AC in the car,' I screamed in my head. But, of course, I was as usual talking only to myself.

'Please take me to Café Greco. You don't have to wait; I can make it back on my own,' I said curtly to Madhav, our driver.

The car stopped just around the corner of the chocolatier-cum-coffee shop. I walked in, and was immediately hit with the thick aroma of chocolate. For an instant I smiled. I had almost forgotten what that was like. I took it all in, and stopped for a moment to commit this moment to memory, trying to erase some of the painful ones of the past. I often did this—replace one memory with another, as in a game of cards, but so far, the dark memories had persisted, if not grown in dimension.

'One spicy hot chocolate with a tinge of cinnamon. Add to that one barbecued chicken in focaccia bread. I'll be in the corner.'

'The order will be placed under whose name, Ma'am?'

'That would be Anjali...Oh, sorry, no. Ankita.'

That hadn't happened in a really long time: for over five years and three months, to be precise. I turned twenty-five last month, and two children are all I have to show for the last six years. After the incident, I haven't been able to write—my only dream since I was seven.

I have had to shut down my past but, for some reason, the memory of it is stronger today than on most days. Shutting down thoughts of the past was my way of dealing with life since compartmentalizing is the only way I can survive. I brought myself back to the present, and tried to focus on the book I had brought with me, *A Clockwork Orange*, but Anthony Burgess wasn't helping either. All this 'You could viddy him thinking about that while he puffed away at his cancer,' just multiplied thoughts of Arpit who was burned into my brain as if with a hot iron.

∽

It had all been too perfect, just that I didn't know it then. When I was in Class XI, I heard through friends and, of course, Aditi, my then-best friend, that Arpit was interested. It's not that I didn't want a boyfriend. I guess every girl does, but I had more to do than most girls—I had to write a book, score 97 per cent, win that scholarship, and travel the world. A boyfriend didn't figure in my life, not right now at least.

I really noticed him for the first time only at the school toppers' ceremony. He was the star, our National Tennis Champion, yet he wasn't cocky like the others. When he went up to the stage to receive the prize, the entire school cheered for him. I wondered what made a guy like Arpit stop to speak to the ordinary old me that day.

Arpit

I *had* to stop by her and congratulate her. Today was my golden chance. If I didn't do it today, I wouldn't be able to do it later. She always minded her own business and never mingled with the others. Today, I had a reason to talk to her. Ankita Labroo had topped her division and had also won a scholarship. She wasn't like the others; you never saw her idling away her time, she didn't play sports. Everything about her was soft, even the way she looked. Her beauty was understated, nothing screamed for attention, yet, all put together, she had the prettiest, gentlest features that I had ever seen.

Anjali

My heart stopped when he came up to me and said, 'Congratulations,' with a shy smile. My normally sharp and agile brain froze. I couldn't understand why, but I guessed it was because I had never imagined that we might one day speak to each other. All I could do was say, 'Thank you'. When he walked away, his lithe frame, his hazel-coloured eyes and his floppy hair remained etched in my mind. Everything about him made me feel tingly and, at the same time, numb.

It seems that we were destined to meet that day. After the awards ceremony, all the winners had to assemble for a photograph. 'Anjali, please stand next to Arpit,' screamed the photographer and I hesitatingly stepped beside him, my heart stuck in my throat.

Arpit

She smelt like no one else. It was a tingling fresh mix of musk, jasmine and vetiver. I knew then that more than anything else, I wanted to get to know her, hold her, kiss her and share her secrets.

Anjali

I didn't want to stand next to him. I felt strangely nervous. Thankfully, the photo session was soon over and before Arpit could say anything, I walked away quickly, only to see my sister running towards me.

'Didi, you are the rock star. Come, Papa and Mamma are waiting in the corridor,' chirped Sakshi.

'Anjali beti, we are so proud of you. My colleagues will now say that every daughter should be like Mrs Labroo's,' said Mamma, a proud grin on her face.

'Let her be, Mrs Labroo. She has one more year to finish school. Let her enjoy her final days before she conquers the world,' said Papa with a chuckle. He was all for living life at a languid pace.

Arpit

Anjali walked away even before the photographer said, 'Disperse'. I was dejected, but I guess it was okay, because there wasn't much I could have said to her anyway. I did have her number, courtesy Prakash, but it felt odd to text her when we hadn't shared even one sentence. Dhruv and Prakash caught me looking at her disappearing frame, and I guess my eyes gave it all away.

'Idiot! You are not going to get any attention from her. She has scored 95 per cent; student and girls like that don't get involved...at least not with men like us,' teased Dhruv.

I just gave them a dirty look, a friendly whack on their buttocks and they both walked away with a laugh.

For the next few days, my life was a whirlwind of tuitions, tennis practice, and squabbles with my parents who thought I wasn't studying enough. It's wasn't easy to maintain grades and to play tennis for the country. I wanted to be in the India U-19 team again, and the selection process was just a few months away. In the midst of all this pressure-laden stuff, she was my only moment of relief. I thought about her constantly. Once or twice I caught her walking down the corridor and she smiled demurely at me. Little did she know how much those smiles meant to me!

Anjali

I desperately wanted to speak to him but I also felt overwhelmingly scared to do so. It was the oddest combination of feelings, in my otherwise-sorted-out mind. But the confusion wasn't to last and Aditi was the reason I let myself be swayed.

'Anju, come with me. I have to go meet Prakash. Even Arpit will be there; apparently he has the biggest crush on you,' said Aditi with a sneaky smile.

'No, I have to head home, my sister will be waiting downstairs. You carry on...'

'How can you do this to me? You're my best friend, aren't you interested in my love life? Can't you at least pretend?' shrieked Aditi, who appeared to be truly offended by my lack of response.

I didn't need much convincing. I did feel guilty for not spending enough time with her. She was my best (and only friend) and then there was Ankit.

'Okay. Come on, let's go,' I said, giving in.

Arpit

I had to wait for Aditi and Prakash to slip away for a while and then get back. The things we do for our friends, I thought, angry with myself for getting involved in their silly love affair. And then I saw Anjali walking alongside Aditi. Oh, my! I couldn't believe my luck.

'We will be back. The two of you get to know each

other,' chimed Aditi, as she left a shocked Anjali by my side and disappeared with Prakash.

Anjali

I wanted to hit her for doing this and as I stood there face to face with him, the most awkward silence ensued.

'Hi!' a text on my phone announced.

I looked at Arpit and I saw a smile forming at the corners of his lips. 'How do you even have my number? Why are you messaging me, when I'm standing right here?' I asked him.

'We are in the same batch so it's not hard to get your number. I thought an SMS might help break the ice since we can't seem to talk to each other,' said Arpit.

'Hello!' I texted back. His phone beeped when he saw my message, his face lit up and I was standing right there to see it.

'This is so weird,' I said aloud.

'I know,' said Arpit.

'Do you want to grab a mug of coffee sometime? Or hot chocolate? I know you like that,' said Arpit.

'What? We don't even know each other. How do you know what I like?' I asked.

'I can guess, can't I?' said Arpit with a smile. 'Would you like to have a hot chocolate with me sometime?'

Before he could respond, Aditi came and dragged me away.

'You came too soon. He was just starting to speak to

me. He didn't...' My words echoed in my mind.

'Yes? Next week?' Arpit's message beeped in.

Anjali

I don't know what made me say yes. The feeling was too disturbing for me to ignore it. I wondered whether this was how Aditi felt about Prakash.

Arpit too surprised me. I was gearing myself for a cocky jock-type boy but he wasn't like that at all—he was shy, kind and polite. Given his popularity in school, he could so easily have been a jerk, but he seemed very sweet instead.

Anjali

My life has been a whirlwind ever since Arpit walked into it and no matter how much I try, I don't know how to silence those insistent feelings. The more time I spend with him, the more I realize how much I like him. He is a great listener, and seems so comfortable in his own skin. Unlike the other boys in school, he never tries hard to be cool, and he never shows off. Also, I know he genuinely likes me. I can tell that by the way he is always so attentive towards me, by the way he is so shy around me, and most of all by the way that he looks at me.

Arpit

Life was hard, I hardly ever saw her. With each passing

day, I began to fall even more deeply in love. I wanted to touch her, hold her, kiss her.

'I wish we were in the same class. I miss you,' I messaged her during the psychology class. Like always, she was on my mind.

'I miss you more,' she replied.

I was still beaming from the SMS when I stepped out to go for the next class. As I turned right, Anjali tugged at left my arm, gave me a peck on the cheek and ran away. I blushed and the tingling feeling was back again. She had never kissed me before.

I stood on the sidewalk messaging Anjali. As usual, Dhruv poked in his big nose.

'Are you going to just keep messaging her...or will you do something?' Dhruv taunted me.

'You need to chill out, man; like freaking calm down, brother,' I retorted, irritated.

'Yeah, right. She is not going to let you even close to her. I've already had a bet with Prakash. All you can do is watch some porn and FANTASIZE about getting her.'

I should have kept my cool, but Dhruv got to me that day. Lately, he had been making it his mission to tease me about Anjali. I should have asked him to stop, or better yet made him stop (I was after all stronger than him) but I didn't want to get into anything messy and risk suspension. The school authorities had recently really clamped down on bullying, so I shrugged off my anger and walked away. The truth was that I didn't really like Dhruv. I hung out with him because he was my tennis partner, but that's where my friendship with him ended. Though he was annoying as hell, he wasn't a bad guy. It's just that he had a bad attitude towards girls. Like most of the other boys in school, he thought the only reason to get with girls was to have some action. I had dated a few girls in school, and I didn't mind getting physical with them; but it wasn't the only reason why I was with them. Moreover, it felt different with Anjali. I loved her, and that was the truth of it. My stupid friends didn't understand that, and they probably wouldn't even if I tried to explain it to them.

Anjali

'It's getting late now. My parents will wonder what I'm up to. I'm in the bathroom, I should go...' I said to Arpit.

'Wait...tell me what are you wearing.'

'T-shirt and shorts. I have to go now. Bye. Good night,' I said, embarrassed.

'Don't go, yaar. Give me a kiss before you go, na.'

'Muuuaaah,' I said with a laugh and hung up the phone.

Arpit: You must be looking sexy in that night suit. Do you have teddy bears on it by any chance?

Arpit: I feel like running my fingers all over you now. I really do.

Anjali: AAARPPPIIITT!!!!

It's not as if we hadn't kissed or touched each other before. We had, and though it was the first time for me, I had really enjoyed it. Sometimes, I couldn't understand myself: till just a few months ago, I didn't have a boyfriend and I hadn't felt the need for one either. Now that I did have one, I wanted to be around him all the time and do other things too. Just the thought of all this embarrassed me immensely. I never imagined that I would be like this!

Arpit

She has this smell. It's her hair; the shampoo, or whatever. It drives me mad and I want to go deeper. Sometimes just touching her turns me on. It's not that I have dirty thoughts about her, I don't. Well, okay fine, occasionally I do. I just want to run my fingers all over her...I like it when she touches me too and when she teases me with her soft fingers. Oh my God! I have to meet her ASAP. All these thoughts are driving me crazy.

Anjali

I desperately wanted to meet him. He had stirred something within me, and it wasn't a mere tickle anymore. It was a quiet fire and I wanted to feel him, touch him, kiss him, and maybe something more too.

As soon as we met, we kissed each other passionately. He felt me up, unbuttoning my shirt and grazing me with his tongue. It felt nice and I knew that he wanted me to touch him too. As he was leading my hand towards the zipper of his pants, he took out his phone and took a couple of pictures and shot a short video. It unnerved me but, in a weird way, I enjoyed it. It made me feel that he desired me, the way I desired him.

'It's just something to look at when I don't meet you for days. It's just for me,' he said, kissing me all over.

Anjali

I actually don't know what to write. Imagine, a writer who has no words! All I can say is that I love him and it feels amazing. I thought love would be distracting, but it's not. It makes me feel more complete, more driven, more energized. I work at lightning speed because I want to see him, spend as much time with him as possible. In his presence, I feel a rush like I've never felt before. It's better than the one I get when I see good marks, or when I won that prize. It's a different sort of rush, and it's the most amazing feeling in the world.

Arpit

A few days later, Dhruv took a jab at me again because of Ankita. I let it go even though I knew that this problem could simply be solved if I showed him the video. That would shut him up forever. But then again, the video was meant for me and only me. I didn't want other boys watching it, and seeing my girlfriend like that. I just had to tolerate that idiot, and if it got too much, then...well, I would just have to break some rules.

After tennis practice, Dhruv piped up again.

'I knew you wouldn't be able to do anything. You'll

just be another fling for her,' Dhruv said loudly so that the other guys could hear him.

'I'm not just another fling for her. She's never had a fling. She's not the type,' I said, tired after a long practice, and irritated too, because I had lost a match to him.

'Dude, why are *you* the school champion? Especially if you can't even do anything with her except carry her backpack and water bottle,' Dhruv teased, determined, it seemed, to piss me off.

'Shut the fuck up,' I said quietly. And then, under my breath, 'If only you knew, brother.'

Dhruv looked at me with raised eyebrows.

'You've done it, haven't you? Otherwise you would've smacked me by now. I *know* you have. Don't lie. What has Mr Goody done with Mrs Goody?' he said with a laugh.

Dhruv grabbed my phone out of my hand, and ran off with it. I ran after him, cursing out loud.

I heard him laughing loudly, and he threw my phone back to me. 'That clip was so hot, dude. It's made me so horny,' taunted Dhruv.

I rolled up my sleeves, ready to give him the thrashing of a lifetime but before I could beat him up, he ran away, leaving a cloud of dust in my face.

Anjali

'What the hell have you done?' Aditi screamed at me as soon as I walked into the classroom.

I was taken aback by her strange outburst. 'What are

you talking about? What have I done?'

'You let him take a video? Prakash told me about it... How could you?' Aditi hissed at me.

I felt nauseous; I could not breathe. I had to hold on to the banister to stop myself from falling. I couldn't think straight, and my mind was a haze of thoughts—the lab, the video, Ankit unbuttoning my shirt and feeling me up, him pulling out his phone—was all this on the video? And who had seen it? How could Arpit do this? I didn't know what to do or how to react. Even though I couldn't believe it, there was only one way that Aditi could have come to know about the video.

Arpit

The tennis practice had gone well, and after weeks of practice my backhand lob was finally improving. The coach too was in a good mood, and said my serve too was improving, and that now, possibly, it might be the best serve in the country. After the coach left, I quickly gathered my stuff. Even though the others were still practicing, I was leaving. I couldn't wait to meet her. But then, I saw her walking towards me across the tennis court. I laid down my rackets and ran towards her, overjoyed to see her here.

The first thing I noticed was the angry, horrified look on her face.

'What the fuck is wrong with you, Arpit? How *could* you? Why did you share the video?' she screamed at me.

I was dumbfounded.

'But I didn't share it with anyone,' I said, totally confused.

'Don't you dare lie to me! How could you?' shouted Anjali.

And then I remembered. That asshole Dhruv running down the field with my phone.

'Only Dhruv saw it...And that too maybe. He stole my phone...I...I couldn't help it. I don't know what you are getting worked up about,' I said feebly.

She just stared at me, completely aghast.

Phhatak! That's all I heard. I was blinded for a second and my ears rang. Anjali had slapped me and stormed off.

It took me a second to register what had happened. I realized only when I heard the boys laughing. I was pissed off. How dare she slap *me* in front of all my mates?

'How could she slap you? Who does she think she is? Let's teach that bitch a lesson.' Dhruv grabbed my phone from me, and before I could react or even snatch the phone back, he sent the video clip to his number. I should have fought with him to delete the video, but I didn't have the presence of mind then. The slap was still ringing in my ears and all I wanted was revenge. No one had ever slapped me, not my parents, nor my coach, how then, dared she? Who did she think she was?

It was Dhruv who made me post the video online. I knew even then that it was a bad idea; but in my burning anger, I wasn't thinking straight. It would teach her the right kind of lesson, he whispered to me, and said that we would leave it online long enough to create a little noise, and we could take it down a few days later.

I didn't know that the video would spread like wildfire, that within hours it would go viral, that it would spread not just through our school, but through the city, the state, and even the country. The video made national headlines, it got our school principal fired, it got Anjali and me expelled, though it was no fault of hers. I had never imagined, not in my wildest dreams, that a simple video shot for shits and giggles, would ruin her life and mine.

I couldn't forgive myself. How could I have let this happen? I was the star of the school, the tennis champion, the guy everyone looked up to. And now...I was just an asshole who had ruined a good girl's life. After the video spread, Anjali disappeared. No one knew where she had gone, and as for me—a few days before the national selection—the police came to arrest me. My father stood watching them take me away; he didn't say a word. When I saw the hurt and disgust in his eyes, I felt completely defeated. I knew that this was a match I had lost even before I had played it. I saw Anjali at the police station with her parents. She wasn't crying—her eyes were empty, and the sparkle in them was gone. In that moment, the seriousness of my crime struck me and my mind became completely numb. How could I have done this to her? To us? To our love?

∞

'Ma'am, your hot chocolate has gone cold. Would you like us to warm it up for you?' asked the server.

'Yes, please. The sandwich too,' I said.

After passing Class XII, I was married off to Rajat. The only reason he agreed to marry me was because he too has his own secrets. He was implicated in a banking fraud case which he managed to get squashed, and he is gay. After the wedding, I realized that he had no interest in me. I was just his cover-up, like he was mine.

Taking a look at the bill, I see Anjali written on it—a name I had not seen in six long years. After the scandal, I had had to change my name. Because of a few minutes' indiscretion, in a matter of weeks, years of my life had been erased. From Anjali, I became Ankita, and Anjali ceased to exist.

∽

Acknowledgements

I would like to thank the folks at Channel V (Star India Pvt. Ltd) for getting this project on board. As always I want to extend my greatest thanks to my family and friends for being there with me through the difficult and often lonely writing process. If it wasn't for them this book, or any others for that matter would never have been written.

In particular, I would like to thank my parent, Vishwapati and Mona Trivedi for providing a safe and nurturing environment for me to live and work in.

This book is an important one—it got me back in the writing mode after a long hiatus, for that I will be ever grateful.